In the Face of Darkness

"¡adelante!"
"Onward!"

To
Lucy

IN THE
FACE
OF
DARKNESS

THE HEROIC LIFE AND HOLY DEATH
of
Mother Luisita

Sr Timothy Marie O.C.

BY SISTER TIMOTHY MARIE KENNEDY, O.C.D.

Aug 31, 2019

SOPHIA INSTITUTE PRESS
Manchester, New Hampshire

Sophia Institute Press
Box 5284, Manchester, NH 03108
1-800-888-9344

www.SophiaInstitute.com

Sophia Institute Press® is a registered trademark of Sophia Institute.

Library of Congress Cataloging-in-Publication Data
To come.

First printing

"For greater things you were born."

—Venerable Mother María Luisa Josefa of the
Most Blessed Sacrament, O.C.D., "Mother Luisita"

To the faith-filled people of Mexico who endured untold suffering during the religious persecution of the 1920s and 1930s; to Cardinal Timothy Manning and Mother Margarita María Hernández, O.C.D., who, moved by the Holy Spirit, established the Carmelite Sisters of the Most Sacred Heart of Los Angeles; and to Archbishop José Gomez, Archbishop of Los Angeles, protector, advocate, and defender of religious freedom in the twenty-first century.

Contents

Appendices

Foreword

I first "met" Mother Luisita when I came to Los Angeles in the spring of 2010. A friend told me about her, describing her as a virtually unknown local saint. I became captivated by the story of Venerable Mother María Luisa Josefa of the Most Blessed Sacrament. A wife and widow from a privileged background, she became a contemplative nun who ran hospitals and orphanages for the poor before being driven underground and eventually into exile during the bloody persecution of the Mexican Church in the 1920s. She was welcomed to Los Angeles, along with thousands of refugees from the violence in Mexico, by my predecessor, Archbishop John J. Cantwell.

Mother Luisita and her Sisters ministered throughout the Archdiocese of Los Angeles, working without pay, teaching children, and caring for the poor and the sick. Working closely with local pastors, the Sisters shared in the poverty of those they served and responded with calm and grace to the occasional flare-ups of anti-immigrant prejudice they faced, even at times from fellow Catholics.

The émigré gifts that Mother Luisita brought to this city and country are still bearing fruits. She founded the Carmelite Sisters of the Most Sacred Heart of Los Angeles, a unique and authentic offshoot of the ancient Carmelite tradition that joins the Carmelite thirst for union with God with a demanding apostolate to the poor.

The Carmelites continue to shape the spiritual identity and moral character of the Church in Los Angeles, and their friendship and collaboration is one of the blessings of my ministry as archbishop. Over the years, my devotion to their foundress has continued to deepen.

In my inaugural homily, I invoked her witness as a kind of "evangelical key" to understanding our mission in Los Angeles:

> Venerable Mother Luisita would tell everyone: "For greater things you were born!" That's it, my friends! That's the good news we are called to proclaim to our city, to our country, throughout this continent and world! Each of us has been made for love and for great and beautiful things. There is no soul that God does not long to touch with this message of His love! And He wants to touch those souls through us.

Later, I took these words of Mother Luisita for the title of my second pastoral letter, on the Incarnation and God's plan of love, which calls all of us to the "greater things" of being saints—holy men and women living as children of God in the image of Jesus Christ.

I have come to see Mother Luisita as a saint sent to the Church in the Americas especially for these times. The background to her witness is the persecution of the Church by the Mexican government in the years following the revolution.

It has always troubled me that this period in the history of the Americas seems largely forgotten. When people write about the "murder ideologies" of the twentieth century, they speak of

Nazism and atheistic communism in Europe, China, and southeast Asia. They seem not to know that closer to home and just a generation ago, thousands of Mexicans, some as young as teenagers, were imprisoned, tortured, and murdered in the name of an atheist-socialist ideology.

It is curious, too, that Catholic religious-freedom advocates in the United States invoke as patrons the martyrs of England's anti-Catholic purges in the sixteenth century, great saints such as More, Becket, and Campion. They seem unaware of the martyrs who fell to an anti-Catholic regime just decades ago, not far from our southern border, heroic witnesses such as Miguel Pro, Anacleto González Flores, José Sánchez del Rio, and Luis Magaña Servín.

In Mexico, Catholics faced not an adulterous, power-hungry king, but an atheist tyrant, Plutarco Elías Calles. They called him "the Butcher," and he boasted of the priests he had killed and of his plans to wipe Christianity from Mexicans' consciousness in a single generation. And he almost succeeded. Across the country, churches, seminaries, and convents were desecrated and destroyed. Public worship was outlawed, leaving tabernacles empty of the presence of Christ for the first time in nearly four hundred years. Hundreds of priests were tortured and killed during the persecution—many strung up on poles along the highways, others shot while celebrating Mass.

In this fine book, Sister Timothy Marie, O.C.D., sets Mother Luisita's witness squarely in the context of this reign of terror that drove faithful Catholics underground and eventually forced thousands to take refuge in the United States.

We know from historians such as Jesuit Father Wilfrid Parsons that Mother Luisita's agriculture-rich home state of Jalisco was the site of some of the bloodiest attacks and the most courageous resistance. In his *Mexican Martyrdom* (1936), Parsons tells how government forces in Jalisco's capital, Guadalajara, rounded up forty elderly men and women and marched them to the cemetery in the dead of night and shot them. Their crime was going to Mass.

He tells another story about a heroic Jalisco priest, Father Francisco Vera. There is a harrowing photograph that you can still find on the Internet, distributed back then by government propagandists. It shows Father Vera in his priestly vestments and biretta facing a firing squad. Four soldiers train their rifles on him as he looks them in the eye, hands folded in prayer.

This was the climate in Jalisco in 1927, where Sister Timothy Marie begins her story of Mother Luisita. She tells of government soldiers killing and looting in the hill country, as Mother Luisita, quietly and incognito, boards a train in Guadalajara, bound for Nogales, Arizona. She celebrated her sixty-first birthday on that train, as she made her way finally to Los Angeles, arriving on June 24, 1927, the feast of the Sacred Heart.

Sister Timothy Marie writes with a novelist's ear for dialogue and an eye for detail. Her storytelling brings out the complex human character of the saint and the times she lived in. This book is hagiography for our times, the way it should be written. And these pages are rich with words drawn from Mother Luisita's own writings.

Much of Mother Luisita's spiritual legacy was handed down in the form of letters written on the backs of envelopes and scraps of paper and carried secretly across the border to her Sisters still ministering in Mexico. She wrote in code to avoid giving away their hiding places. In her letters, the persecuted Church is called "grandmother"; my predecessor, Archbishop Cantwell, is "Papa Juanito" or "grandfather."

The saint you will meet in these pages is a shrewd, practical foundress, a mystic of everyday life, and above all a wise observer and keen guide of souls. She had a wry sense of humor worthy of her spiritual mother, the great Saint Teresa of Avila, once telling a young Sister: "Try not to neglect your spiritual reading, prayer, and examination of conscience—and have some fun, also."

We find in Mother Luisita a deep appreciation for the wisdom of Saint Thérèse of Lisieux's "Little Way" as well. She lived in close intimacy with God, aware that she was always in His presence. She taught her Sisters to have a rock-solid trust in God's loving providence and urged them to abandon themselves to seek His will in everything.

"May you use every day of your life to love Him, to serve Him, and to thank Him for the love He has for you," she said. "May His will be done. Place yourself in His hands, for you are His, and He will allow to happen whatever is most pleasing to Him."

Mother Luisita told her Sisters that their holiness and salvation would be found in serving Jesus in the poor and the sick and in trying to perform even the smallest labors of daily life for the love of God. "All for You, my God," was her prayer. She urged her Sisters to stay faithful to their daily duties and work for "little victories" over their selfishness and weaknesses. "Be a little better, more and more each day," she would say.

Always, Mother Luisita would call her Sisters, and all of us, to those greater things of God. "For greater things you were born," she once wrote. "Pray for me. I want to be what I should be." And what she should be—what God made each of us to be—is a great saint.

She wrote these words long before the Second Vatican Council would restore the "universal call to holiness" as the vital mark of Christian identity. Mother Luisita is one of the prophets of holiness whom God raised up in those decades before the Council. Her life and works deserve to be studied alongside Venerable

IN THE FACE OF DARKNESS

Madeleine Delbrêl, Servant of God Dorothy Day, Blessed Charles de Foucauld, and others from those years who called us to live as saints in everyday life, with our hearts open to the sufferings of the poor and the forgotten.

Sister Timothy Marie has given us an important book for this moment in the Church.

Reading history through the lives of the saints, we can see that they are the true agents of history, that God raises up saints in every time and place to bear the light of Christ and scatter the darkness that would turn our hearts from God and His plan for our lives and the world.

The great danger we face today is "de-sacralization." We live now in a technological society that closes our eyes to God's presence and to the transcendent dimensions of reality and human existence. With the loss of God has come the disappearance of the human person and new forms of cruelty and inhumanity that we see all around us in our society.

This is why I believe that Mother Luisita is a saint for these times. She brings us a message of spiritual renewal that begins with interior conversion of the heart and is manifested in works of mercy and compassion. She shows us the way to be contemplatives in the midst of the world's sufferings, living in the presence of God, working to advance the dignity and transcendent destiny of the human person, especially those whom Jesus most identified with—the hungry and the homeless, the sick, the immigrant, and the imprisoned.

At a time when the Church in this country is more and more shaped by the experience of immigrants and refugees from Latin America, Mother Luisita brings us a spirituality that is authentically Hispanic. From out of the darkness of the worst persecution the Church has ever seen in the Americas, she teaches us how to live out heroic Christianity, surrendering ourselves to God's will and living only for Him. "Sorrow precedes joy, fear precedes conviction, weakness precedes strength, and all redounds to the welfare of those who love God," she tells us.

Mother Luisita comes to challenge us, as she challenged her Sisters. And make no mistake, she could be tough in reminding us that God is calling each of us to live our lives beautifully and for Him alone.

Are you becoming a saint? God our Lord has given you a soul for that very purpose, and woe to you if you do not correspond to the graces that He has granted you. You've been especially chosen through the predilection of a great God. Don't be a coward, my daughter. Fight in a manly manner against your passions. Overcome yourself! Seek sanctity through the ordinary duties of daily life, and don't let any occasion that presents itself to you take control of you or have any dominion over you. If you follow this advice, I can assure you that in a very short time you'll gather so much spiritual wealth that even you will be surprised. Don't doubt it. And not with just a little bit of effort, either, but with perseverance. *Adelante*, my daughter! Onward!

I pray that this fine book will introduce many to this unknown saint of Los Angeles and the Americas. May her witness inspire a deep renewal in the Church, through a new commitment to the greater things, to becoming the saints we are born to be.

—Most Reverend José H. Gomez
Archbishop of Los Angeles
December 12, 2018
Feast of Our Lady of Guadalupe

Acknowledgments

I offer my deepest thanks to the many people who supported the writing of this book: to Archbishop José Gomez for his foreword; to Mother Judith Zúniga, our superior general, for allowing me the time and space to pray, research, think, and write; to our gracious Loretto and Casa Sisters, who opened up their beautiful convent as a sacred space for writing; to my Sisters who gave up their precious free time to proofread; and to those Sisters who so charitably assumed extra duties to free me up to write.

My profound appreciation also goes to the valued input of Father John Henry Hanson, O. Praem., and Father Gerard Gonda, O.S.B.; to friends who turned out to be the most talented and amazing proofreaders: Lucia Bartoli, Jo De La Torre, Alice Godfrey, Barbara Hanna, Alanna Psomas, Carlos Tobón, and my talented sister and author, Kathy Kennedy-Tapp. A special word of thanks to Msgr. Francis Weber and Kevin Feeney, past and current archivists of the Archdiocese of Los Angeles, for their help in confirming the names of people and finding correct dates; to David Scott, vice-chancellor of communications in the Archdiocese of Los Angeles, for his enthusiasm and support of the Cause of our Mother Luisita and for his much-appreciated help;

IN THE FACE OF DARKNESS

and to Dan Burke for helping us move forward in the writing, publishing, and promotion of *In the Face of Darkness.*

Most of all, I offer my deepest gratitude to the faithful, courageous Sisters who lived through the turbulent history described in this book.

A Note from the Carmelite Sisters

So many years have passed. Is there anyone who remembers? And who would even want to answer questions about those years spent in the face of darkness? These were some of the thoughts running through our minds as Sister Mary Jeanne and I began our journey up and down the state of California.

In our search for documents and memories, we traveled south on California's Interstate 710 all the way to its end, at the port city of Long Beach. Then we reversed directions and drove north on Interstate 5 to San Francisco, Moraga, and San José. We were thrilled that we had been asked to find out as much as we could about the religious persecution of the 1920s and 1930s in Mexico. More exciting is what we discovered in college archives, in convents of Catholic nuns, and in conversations with the gracious members of the Flores family, who had opened their home to Mexican refugees fleeing the persecution.

We heard countless stories. Thank God: there they were, still waiting for us as if they knew that the time had finally come to be told. Do not think it was easy to bring up memories of the religious persecution in Mexico, of relatives tortured and killed, or of those who were missing and never found. Tears flowed freely down the faces of the people we interviewed, who had fled the persecution in Mexico and found refuge in the United States.

What came forth from our travels is the story of one woman whose dauntless faith withstood obstacle after obstacle as she watched the religious freedom of her homeland, Mexico, crushed yet again by the government.

This is her story—her seventy-year journey from child to married woman, to widow, to foundress of a new community of consecrated women, and finally, to refugee in a foreign country. Based on the results of our research, this book follows her life journey through flashbacks, the method we chose to bring together the documents and memories we discovered. To help the flow of the story, this account has transferred some of her letters (she wrote more than six hundred) into conversations.

In the Face of Darkness is woven from Mother Luisita's letters, testimonies of those who knew her, recollections of her family and others, and documents from the archives and oral tradition of her two communities: the Carmelite Sisters of the Sacred Heart of Mexico and the Carmelite Sisters of the Most Sacred Heart of Los Angeles. The Archdiocese of Guadalajara's presentation of her life of heroic virtue to the Congregation for the Causes of Saints also contributed to this story of Mother Luisita's witness to God's love, providence, and mercy.

She came to be known simply as Mother Luisita, highly respected and deeply loved, known for turning stumbling blocks into stepping stones and for bringing hope to people at the limit of their endurance. She was a woman of faith and courage who boldly said, "Look to God, your soul, and eternity. All the rest is a wisp of smoke."

Even the longest life is short, traversed through mountains and valleys, lights and shadows, laughter and pain. During the

A Note from the Carmelite Sisters

difficult times, when evil seems to obliterate the light, it is then that God raises up people like Mother Luisita to guide us through the darkness.

Sister Mary Jeanne Coderre, O.C.D., and
Sister Timothy Marie Kennedy, O.C.D.

Introduction

Saints give us hope. When we read stories about them, we discover that lives of integrity and virtue are possible even in today's frenzied world. The saints raise the bar of gospel living.

This story is about an amazing person who has something to teach all of us—Venerable Mother María Luisa Josefa of the Most Blessed Sacrament, known simply as Mother Luisita. Her example pierces through today's culture as a guiding beacon of God's light and grace. The following points were submitted to the Vatican's Congregation for the Causes of Saints as her Cause for beatification and sainthood began:

- She lived during a time of great religious persecution, and it was in this atmosphere that Mother's heroic virtues were revealed and her reputation for holiness began to take form.
- Her spirit of prayer transformed her into an authentic contemplative who found God in everything, and at the same time, her distinct and effective love reached out to the poor and needy.
- She was an extraordinary woman who knew how to live deeply her Christian vocation in both the married state and in her religious life.

• Her wish was to meet the greatest needs of the times, the education of poor children and the care of the sick lacking financial means, through the establishment of her religious institute.[1]

Mother Luisita is the foundress of two communities—the Carmelite Sisters of the Sacred Heart of Mexico and the Carmelite Sisters of the Most Sacred Heart of Los Angeles.

This is her story.

---

[1] These excerpts are taken from the *Positio Super Virtutibus* submitted to the Congregation for the Causes of Saints. The *Positio* is a collection of documents used in the process by which a person is declared Venerable, the second of the four steps on the path to sainthood. The four steps are: Servant of God, Venerable, Blessed, and Saint.

In the Face of Darkness

Chapter 1

The List

*You must not see yourself as being alone. On the contrary,
now you are more accompanied than ever before because
Our Lord is always with those who suffer. Talk to Him.
Trust Him with all your sufferings. Tell Him about your
doubts and abandon yourself entirely into His Hands.*

—Undated letter to Sister Refugio during
the religious persecution in Mexico

No one dared to venture outside the locked gates of their homes.
Everyone was in shock, terrified. People spoke in hushed whispers.
Birds stopped singing, as if they, too, were reeling in disbelief and
horror at what was happening in their beautiful city of Guadalajara, once so alive with laughter, music, and rich Mexican culture.

The Cristero Uprising had come to Guadalajara.

War changes everything. It is difficult to say which is
worse—fear of the unknown or fear of the known; the stress and
fear that comes with the threat of war or the war itself, with the
uncertainties of day-to-day living during wartime. Not knowing
is acutely stressful. The unanswered questions remain curled up
like a tight ball in the pit of the stomach. How close to home
will the battles be? Will we have enough provisions to get by?

IN THE FACE OF DARKNESS

General Jesús María Ferreira, chief of the military zone of the state of Jalisco, Mexico, only six weeks earlier had ordered the reconcentration of all persons living in the surrounding Los Altos hills. He drove these rural people out of their homes and took over their ranches and everything in them for the federal soldiers to pillage. They were forced to travel to the plazas of selected cities, arriving no later than the first week in May 1927. Guadalajara's plaza was among the plazas selected.

To assess the extent of the damage that General Ferreira caused, one had only to open the front door and walk a few steps onto the street. Driven from their ranches, groups of displaced people had entered the city, pushed forward by the sheer numbers moving together toward their destination. More and more people crowded into the plaza and the outlying avenues. An exhausted silence accompanied their forced trek over the hills to Guadalajara. Thousands had already arrived, and thousands more were on their way.

Mexican families opened their doors to these uprooted men, women, and children. They shared their homes and their sustenance, but there was not enough housing for the displaced people swarming into the city, nor enough food or sufficient sanitation to meet their needs, causing a stench to settle upon their beautiful city.

As the plaza clock struck twelve, safe within the locked gates of one of the homes, a woman knelt on the tiled patio floor, hands clasped and head bowed. Needing to make her decision right away, she had discreetly left the others inside the house to be alone with her thoughts. When she looked up, her furrowed forehead and tightly drawn lips belied her gentle spirit.

She couldn't shake off the atrocities she had seen and heard about, especially the story of the three thousand, faith-filled

Mexican women who had taken their stand on the plaza of Santa Familia Church in a suburb of Mexico City. These heroines had formed a human barrier in front of the church to protest and stop the forced removal of their priests.

When mounted police arrived at the church, they sprayed fire hoses at full force into the crowd of women and galloped into the throng, trampling many of these valiant heroines. Five thousand more fearless Mexican women soon arrived to form a new, larger human barrier. Many of these women were also trampled and bludgeoned.

The Franciscan Sisters from San Martín de Bolaños were ambushed by soldiers and carried away on horseback. They were returned a month later and refused to speak to anyone about their ordeal.

Her own recent experiences came unbidden into her mind —the times she and the other Carmelite Sisters were forced to make quick escapes over rooftops or had been walled in to protect themselves from the soldiers.

Her eyes expressed inner fear and indecision because her life and the lives of the fifty-five Carmelite Sisters in her fledgling community were in imminent danger. Even now the federal soldiers were combing the city searching for them, and her options had finally run out. With her hands covering her face, she breathed deeply and waited expectantly for an answer to her prayer.

Lord, what do You want us to do?

She knew the government was also searching for her family —the wealthy de la Peñas—and other families of the upper class. The government planned to strip them of their inheritances and businesses, in fact, all of their money—whatever they could acquire—to fuel their war against Catholics in the state of Jalisco, Mexico, in the early 1920s.

IN THE FACE OF DARKNESS

What is our next step?

Kneeling on the tiled patio, Mother Luisita came to understand what she must do next. Courage arose within her. With the "determined determination" advocated by Saint Teresa of Avila, Mother Luisita stood up, squared her shoulders, and walked purposefully back to the house. She had come to her decision.

I must escape. My name is on the list.

Chapter 2

Three Tickets, Please

Have serenity even if the world is tumbling down. God
Our Lord is with you, so don't fear anything but sin.

—Letter to Mother Elena, 1934

Mother Luisita and two other Carmelite Sisters spent their last night in Mexico at the home of Mariquita, her younger sister. Early the following morning, Mother Luisita stepped onto the veranda and breathed in the cool air as if to capture the essence of her beloved Mexico to store in her heart. Her clammy, trembling hands revealed the inner turmoil within her.

She heard soft crying in the next room. It was Mariquita. Mother Luisita opened her arms wide and embraced her. "Hush, Mariquita, hush now. Everything will turn out all right. You'll see. For now we suffer and wait, pray and expect. We're all in God's hands. There is no better place that we can be. You know that."

Mother Luisita held on tightly and let her sister purge herself of the built-up emotions of the past year. It had to come sooner or later. "Let's sing. How about a hymn? Which one?"

Still no answer.

IN THE FACE OF DARKNESS

Holding her sister in a firm embrace and rocking her back and forth gently, she softly sang one of their favorite hymns: "O María, Madre mía, o consuelo del mortal ..."[2] She sang all six verses. Rather, she prayed it. When she felt Mariquita's body finally begin to relax, Mother Luisita whispered in her ear, "Mariquita, every morning and night remember to consecrate your family to the Sacred Heart of Jesus. As the hymn says, our Blessed Mother will conquer Satan. She will, Mariquita! She will! Peace! God is with us!"

"The blood ... the screams. Luisita ... the screams—will they ever stop?"

"Only God knows, Mariquita. Only God knows." She sighed and pulled out her small, worn rosary. Holding it up, she said, "This is our weapon."

Her sister finally stopped crying. Mother Luisita continued. "Mariquita, I'd like to meet everyone in the dining room in about half an hour. I'm almost finished packing. I'd like to be alone for a while."

Mariquita nodded. She understood Luisita's need to be alone. Everyone in the de la Peña family respected Luisita's deeply interior temperament. Mariquita had watched Luisita's life unfold for many years now, and she admired and respected her older sister's path, an obedient and rugged way of life marked by humble service to the less fortunate.

"Thank you, Mariquita." She added the traditional Carmelite words of gratitude, "May God reward you," and walked back to the bedroom. Placing her suitcase on the bed, she checked it a final time.

[2]"O María, Madre Mia" is a much-loved, traditional Mexican hymn to our Blessed Mother.

Three Tickets, Please

How I wish Father Pedrito were here to advise me.[3]
Father Pedro Heriz of Saint Elias, O.C.D., was the Carmelite priest who had taken her new community under his wing and provided support and spiritual direction. He was from the Catalonia Province of the Discalced Carmelites in Spain and was authorized to establish new Carmelite communities in Arizona and Mexico and to oversee all the Carmelite communities in Mexico. Father Pedro was a guardian angel to Mother Luisita.

Caught in Mexico's sociopolitical, religious persecution of Catholics, Mother Luisita and her fifty-five Carmelite Sisters were quietly and steadfastly defying the unjust laws of President Plutarco Elías Calles. The Sisters' daily work was plagued by the need to be watchful, lest they be caught by federal soldiers.

So what if their newly opened schools and orphanage had been closed and the hospital was now a federal army hospital? They simply used their common sense and formed an underground network that sprang up overnight. Classes were now held in stables, in fields, and in private homes.

---

[3] Mother Luisita began her community in Atotonilco on December 24, 1904, and Father Pedro, vicar provincial of the Catalonian Carmelites, who was in Jalisco in 1905, helped her with his wise and prudent spiritual direction. In 1920, he was instrumental in providing the Carmelite formation of the new community. During the persecution, while Mother Luisita was in California, Father Pedro was in Washington, D.C., and in Arizona. Through his letters, he helped her to maintain the Carmelite charism of the exiled community in the United States as well as the community members who remained in Mexico. After returning to Spain, he died a martyr on November 11, 1936, at the height of the Spanish Civil War. Antonio Unzueta Echevarria, *Beato Pedro De San Elías: Biografía y Epistolario* (Vitoria-Gasteiz, Spain: Ediciones El Carmen, 2015), 86–94.

IN THE FACE OF DARKNESS

Mother Luisita's new religious congregation, the Carmelite Sisters of the Third Order of Guadalajara, had been officially approved by the Catholic Church only six years earlier, and as foundress of the newly formed community, she took to heart her responsibility to keep them safe.

She continued checking her suitcase.

Everything has to be in here. If anything is left behind, that's where it will have to stay. I don't know how long I'll be gone.

Like an unbridled horse, her mind raced into the future, her thoughts galloping one after the other as she went through the items in her suitcase.

Will I ever come back? How safe will the other Sisters be while I am gone?

She reached down and touched her Carmelite habit. Her tunic and scapular, white coif, large brown rosary beads, crucifix, black veil, and white mantle, were all folded carefully in her suitcase.

Yes, everything is here.

She closed the suitcase.

Today she was wearing a new, simple, classically designed black dress. Just a few weeks ago, she had invited trusted friends over to say good-bye, and they had been appalled when she showed them the long, drab outfits the Sisters were planning to wear on the train to the United States.

"Heavens," they cautioned, "you can't wear that. You'll be discovered for sure in that rag. Trust us. We'll take care of getting you the right outfits. Believe us, Mother, it will help you at the border if you are well dressed." The women exchanged subtle, knowing looks at the mention of the border crossing.

Finally, everything was ready for the journey. Mother Luisita trembled. The initial weighing of the pros and cons of undertaking this perilous trip was over. She had talked it over with

Three Tickets, Please

Monsignor Manuel Alvarado, vicar-general of the Diocese of Guadalajara, who was in charge while Archbishop Francisco Orozco y Jiménez was in hiding. The two other Sisters who were to accompany Mother Luisita, forty-year-old Sister Teresa of Jesus Navarro, her second cousin, and twenty-four-year-old Sister Margarita María of the Sacred Heart Hernández, who had only recently professed her vows, were also packing their suitcases in the next room. Sixty-year-old Mother Luisita was the eldest of the three.

The necessary paperwork was finally completed and the required immunizations received. It hadn't been easy, but with the help of friends, everything was finished in time to board the first available train leaving at noon, Monday, June 20, 1927, from the Guadalajara station.

Calm down. Think logically and use your common sense. Take a deep breath. Relax.

The time was moving too slowly. Mother Luisita knew all too well that government spies lurked in strategic places throughout the city. It was a deadly game of hide-and-seek. Every time she found a private home with good people willing to hide a few Sisters, it would soon become unsafe for them to stay there, and they would have to move on.

Someone had recently told them that Guadalajara had the greatest number of martyrs since January, when the guerilla warfare of the Cristiada intensified in Jalisco.[4] That was six months

---

[4] The Cristiada (1926–1929), also known as the Cristero Uprising, was a widespread struggle in many central-western Mexican states against the secularist, anti-Catholic, and anticlerical

ago. Since then, the Cristeros, with very few guns and no military training, were fighting in the hills as the Sisters prepared to leave the country. They were fighting for everything they held dear: for their religious freedom, for their family, for their friends, for their neighbors, for their priests.

Mother Luisita couldn't bear to think about it. She could still hear the soldier's voice piercing the tranquility of the summer's evening: "I'll trade a priest for a horse, a priest for a horse!"

Soldiers cajoled the people into giving them horses for the army to use. For every horse the soldiers received, one of the priests who had been arrested, beaten, and tortured was handed back in exchange.

A priest for a horse.

Yes, it's time to flee from this place.

Someone knocked on the door.

"*Tía*, may I come in for a minute?"

Mother Luisita looked up. Her nephew and godson José was standing in the doorway. "Come in, José."

José Arámbula was Mariquita's son.

"*Tía*, do you have your tickets?"

She reached for the envelope and held it up.

He continued, "Great! Your train will go through some pretty rugged territory before you reach Los Angeles. I came because I have news! The wash overflowed at the site of that first tunnel in *las barrancas*.⁵ The whole tunnel has caved in. It's impassable

---

policies of the Mexican government. It was the Mexican people's war for religious freedom.

⁵ *Las barrancas*: narrow, winding river gorges, ravines, or canyons. "Some of the heaviest railroad construction ever undertaken was involved in completing the final 102 miles of Southern Pacific's line in Mexico. Volcanic formations of the rugged barrancas

now, so you and the other Sisters will have to transfer to another train there. I'm going with you to see you all safely aboard the second train. It's not right to send you off unaccompanied. Times are dangerous, *Tía.*"

She nodded. "Are you coming to our final meeting in your dining room in a few minutes?"

"Sure, I'll be there."

He wanted to say more but sensed his aunt wanted privacy during these last hours, and he left the room.

Mother Luisita watched José leave. As he closed the door behind him, she began checking her second bag—a well-used, brown leather doctor's bag that contained the very few community items they decided to bring with them to start over in the United States. It had belonged to Doctor Pascual Rojas, her husband, who had died more than thirty years ago in Guadalajara.

Inside this bag was a secret. Mother Luisita was the only one who knew that, hidden deep inside, amid a few documents and letters, some fabric and a couple of books, lay a very small, wooden tabernacle wrapped in the softest fabric she could find. She bent over the bag, reached in with both hands, and parted the fabric until she felt the wood and quietly prayed.

---

were particularly tough. Thirty-two tunnels were bored, and on one section of the work, more than 4,000 Mexican laborers were employed. As part of this through line, 23 miles between Orendain Jct. and Guadalajara were leased from the National Railways of Mexico. On April 17, 1927, the first trains were operated over the 1,095-mile through line from Nogales to Guadalajara, where connection was made for Mexico City." Earl Heath, *Seventy-Five Years of Progress: Historical Sketch of the Southern Pacific* (San Francisco: Southern Pacific Bureau, 1945), chap. 4, http://www.cprr.org/Museum/SP_1869-1944/.

IN THE FACE OF DARKNESS

My Jesus, we carry this tabernacle to California. Don't let anyone find it and take it away from us. When we find a place in the United States that we can call home, I will place it in the best room of the house. Then we will open wide its doors as an invitation to You, my Lord, to come and dwell in it, and we will create a little chapel for You. We will sing Your praises and ask forgiveness for the cruelty taking place, and intercede for Your ravaged people who are at the limit of their endurance. Above all, we will make reparation for the blasphemy and sacrileges against You, my Lord and my God.

Mother Luisita brought a tabernacle to each of her new foundations, but for almost a year now, all the tabernacles within the Catholic churches throughout Mexico were empty. The doors of the churches were locked. President Calles enacted his anticlerical laws on July 31, 1926.[6] Because the Mexican bishops could

---

[6] "Anti-clericalism became state policy in Mexico following the revolution of 1860, when President Benito Juárez issued a decree nationalizing church property, separating church and state, and suppressing religious orders.

"After the revolution of 1910, the New Mexican Constitution of 1917 contained even more drastic anti-clerical provisions. Article 3 called for secular education in schools and prohibited the Catholic Church from engaging in primary education; Article 5 outlawed monastic orders; Article 24 forbade public worship outside the confines of churches; and Article 27 placed restrictions on the right of religious organizations to hold property. Most obnoxious to Catholics was Article 130, which deprived clergy members of basic political rights.

"Many of these laws were resisted by the people. This led to the Cristero Uprising [which formally began in Jalisco in 1927]. The repression of the Catholic Church included the closing of many churches and even the killing and the forced marriage of priests....

"The effects of the war on the Church were profound. While there were 4,500 active priests before the rebellion, in 1934

---

not follow them in good conscience, they suspended all public worship in Mexico and closed all Catholic churches rather than bend the knee to Calles and his ultimatums.

Mother Luisita's eyes revealed no self-pity. They showed no anger or desire for revenge, no depression or melancholy. Her eyes were determined and steady. It was this quiet steadfastness that garnered the reverent respect of the people who knew her. She was a leader now, though not a flamboyant, dynamic one. Rather, she was a quiet light piercing through the darkness with an inviting sweetness that drew people to her with confidence.

She closed her eyes.

Help me to be strong, Lord.

Sister Margarita María called from the next room. "Mother, I've finished packing. May I help you?"

"Thank you, but no. I'm all right. I just finished."

But to herself: *We must move quickly.*

---

only 334 priests were licensed by the government to serve 15 million people, the rest having been eliminated by emigration, expulsion, assassination, and attrition. As many as 10 states were left without even a single priest." "Anti-clericalism," *New World Encyclopedia*, http://www.newworldencyclopedia. org/entry/Anti-clericalism.

Chapter 3

Adelante! Onward!

*Just as a drop of water gets absorbed into the ocean
and becomes part of it, or as wax taken from different
honeycombs is totally melted and then fused into one,
that is the way union with God takes place.*

—Letter to Mother Socorro, 1932

José, Mariquita, and the three Carmelites sat down at the dining room table. José raised his hand and looked toward Mother Luisita.

"Yes, José?"

The Sisters turned toward him.

José stood up and looked at each Sister. "Thank you, each one of you. For everything. We all love you so much! We promise that we'll look after the Sisters remaining here in Guadalajara as best we can while you are gone." His eyes searched the faces of the three Carmelites.

Mother Luisita's chest was tight from her tension, and she could hear her heart pounding. Looking up at her nephew, who was much taller than her diminutive, five-foot-one-inch frame, she replied, "That means more to me than anything, José."

She continued. "That reconcentration order has wrought havoc here."[7]

Sister Teresa added, "Mother, some of the wealthier ranchers paid off the soldiers and stayed on their ranches."

Mother Luisita took a deep breath and answered, "Yes." In a low voice she added, "But most families just don't have that kind of money." She shook her head. "All this overcrowding will surely cause epidemics. We have nowhere to hide. People are afraid to hide us in their homes now. We need to find a new place to hide before any of us are arrested."

She had fire in her eyes. "We'll bring as many as we can to the United States. Don't worry, we'll return when things calm down." She looked at each person, intuiting each one's reactions.

"Sisters," José instructed them, "when you arrive at the train station, you'll meet people of all kinds—police, soldiers, thieves, and others. Be vigilant! Pickpockets have increased. Displaced

---

[7] The Carmelite Sisters lived and worked in the heart of the Cristiada, in the region known as Los Altos, in the state of Jalisco, Mexico. In April 1927, about eight weeks before the Sisters left the country for the United States, General Jesús Ferreira gave the order to concentrate the civilian rural population into cities and to declare the Mexican countryside a war zone. All the rural inhabitants were ordered to concentrate in five plazas, including Guadalajara's. All of the products from the country's ranches, the animals, the fruit orchards, the fields of crops, the land they were on, and the buildings on the land, now belonged to the government. The farmers could no longer support the Cristeros with food from their abundant agricultural fields and orchards. This forced the evacuation that relocated the fifty thousand people who lived within eight hundred thousand square miles. Wilfrid Parsons, S.J., *Mexican Martyrdom* (Rockford, IL: TAN Books, 1936), 36.

people linger. Be on your guard and realize there are spies. Act your parts well! And once you leave Jalisco, don't think that the danger is over. No, you'll be in danger every minute until you reach the United States."

He looked around the table at each of the Sisters. "That's why I'm going with you on the train."

He stood up. "Does anyone have questions?"

Nothing.

He grinned sheepishly. "Can you please not act like nuns? Act like wealthy vacationers! Can you swing your arms a little? Watch me. Walk like this." He walked around the table, demonstrating the swing. "Don't keep looking down when you walk. Little things like that." He held out his hands in front of him widely as if to embrace the entire group. "You'll be fine," he concluded as he gave one of his winning smiles.

The brief meeting over, they all stood up and left. Mother Luisita returned to the bedroom and walked around it, looking in the chest of drawers and the closet one last time to make sure that nothing was left behind.

As she closed the bedroom drapes, she felt a sharp pain in her arm. Rolling up her sleeve, she examined the area of the inoculation that she had received a few weeks ago when she applied for her passport. It was very inflamed.

The expected knock on her door finally came. José walked into the room. Sister Teresa and Sister Margarita María followed him.

"*Tía*, it's time to leave now." He picked up her luggage.

"Keep calm, keep calm," Mother Luisita reminded them quietly. "Remember, don't call each other by our religious names. Just say 'Teresa' or 'Luisita.' No more 'Sister.' Just call me 'Auntie' if you'd like. I'd like you to remember two things. First, God is with us. Don't doubt it! And secondly, there is a beautiful side to everything. Even this." The depth of Mother Luisita's faith and the intensity of her love for God filled her being as she said, "The beauty lies in our faith in God and in the vows we have all made to Him. He is not far away. No, He is right here with us. Only God can sustain us."

There had been a few times before when Mother Luisita's eyes had revealed the fire of divine love blazing within her. For a brief moment, Sister Teresa and Sister Margarita María were let in on the secret of Mother Luisita's spiritual stamina. Her soul was filled with such a love of God that the two Sisters gasped at the intimacy of this encounter with the Divine they were experiencing through her.

"How beautiful it is to be in the hands of God, searching His divine gaze in readiness to do whatever He asks," she whispered, drawing them back into the deepest center of their souls, where, as Saint Teresa affirms, God indeed dwells.

The three women picked up the remaining suitcases and parcels and walked resolutely out the door and onto the street.

As they entered the train station, Mother Luisita blended in as a well-dressed upper-class Mexican lady traveling with two friends on a vacation to Southern California. With her impeccable up-bringing, she was not only fashionable, but elegant with her hair stylishly pulled back into a classic twisted knot.

Sister Margarita María, wearing just-purchased fire-engine-red French heels, walked next to her. Mother Luisita was the first to spot the soldiers. A wave of nausea came over her, and she looked away.

God, give me the strength to do this.

Adelante! Onward!

The soldiers strutted by, carrying loaded rifles. Like birds of prey, they moved in endless circles, their piercing eyes sweeping across the crowd in hopes of identifying someone on their list. Mother's fashionable hat covered her face well.

Lord, don't let them find the gold coins!

Her hands grew clammy and began to tremble. She had tucked away four gold coins, each worth fifty dollars. With two hundred dollars in gold coins, they would find a way to begin again.

After several minutes, the train pulled into the station, emitting spirals of steam with each deafening blast. Brakes squealed and hissed, bringing the locomotive to a standstill. Soon porters appeared and began to transport luggage. They moved the suitcases with large two-wheeled dollies. Strong four-wheeled trolleys moved the trunks and heavier luggage into the baggage car.

A few trusted friends and relatives were waiting discreetly at the station for the Sisters. Luisita's heart almost broke when she saw Margarita María's mother, Conchita, her sister Lucita, and her brother Luis enter the station to say good-bye to her.

Ah, Margarita María. Still so young. This persecution is whisking you into maturity, isn't it?

Mother Luisita had already said her final good-byes to her family the night before. Most of the Carmelite Sisters opted not to risk the trip to the station.

The first call to board finally came.

Her family had purchased first-class tickets for them so they could have more privacy on the train and get through the immigration process at the United States border more easily. As soon as Margarita María joined them, Mother Luisita took the three train tickets and passed one to each of the Sisters, keeping the third one for herself.

Then she quietly showed them another set of envelopes. "Here is another little envelope for you. Open it on the train after we are out of the city." Mother Luisita gave a small envelope to each of the Sisters.

Mother Luisita's gaze met the frightened, yet steady eyes of Teresa and the tearful gaze of Margarita María. Her eyes communicated with theirs.

Adelante! God will provide!

They entered the compartment one by one. Each carried her own bags down the narrow corridor. The train doors closed.

After settling into their seats, Margarita María whispered, "Everybody is so quiet."

Mother Luisita glanced around slowly. She had also noticed that many of the other passengers were especially quiet and extraordinarily discreet. It was only then that she realized that most of the other passengers were probably refugees like themselves who were fleeing for their lives. No one seemed anxious to disclose information that would reveal anything about their identity.

As the train left the station at the height of the humid June heat, its rhythmic chugging steadily increased. The whistle sounded its forlorn call into the sultry June landscape surrounding Guadalajara.

They were finally on their way. Margarita María stood up and opened a window, but a passenger seated near her yelled across the aisle, "Señorita, close your window so the soot and hot coal won't blow into our eyes." She closed the window and looked outside. The steam flowing from the engine was indeed filthy.

In contrast to the many subdued passengers, there were others who were already tipsy, even though it was only noon. Unsteady on their feet, they walked clumsily down the narrow aisle.

Adelante! Onward!

Mother Luisita turned around and saw her nephew José sitting next to a family friend, Lorenzo Valle, a relative of Sister Soledad, also from Los Altos. So, Lorenzo was traveling to an American Jesuit school on the same train. Now, they had two guardian angels looking out for their interests during the journey.

Looking around inconspicuously to reassure herself of their safety aboard this train, Mother Luisita gasped. With her lips moving ever so quietly, she breathed out a barely audible "I don't believe it!"

She looked again.

There, sitting in the seat directly across from her, was one of the daughters of President Calles wearing a Miraculous Medal around her neck. Mother Luisita heard the young girl remark to her companion, "Yes, Father is sending me to the United States to attend Our Lady of the Rosary Catholic School in San Diego, California. I wonder what it is going to be like."

Mother Luisita sighed softly as she remembered that the president's wife had died recently.

Well, there's nothing I can do about it. She will be next to us all the way to Nogales.

She leaned back against the plush seat, which smelled clean and new. This was a brand-new train making its first run from Guadalajara to Nogales.

The Sisters were all very tired — not only physically but, more so, emotionally. They closed their eyes and allowed the rhythmic motion of the steam engine with its monotonous cycles of ups and downs to lull them into much-needed sleep.

After about an hour, Mother Luisita woke up. Margarita María was opening her envelope. She nudged Teresa, who pulled hers out at the same time. Both began reading the message at almost the same moment. It read:

IN THE FACE OF DARKNESS

A thought for the journey—
Form a beautiful and rich tabernacle
for Our Lord within your heart
and then do not let Him go.
In that way,
you will always have Him with you.
Enter within yourself, and meeting Him,
tell Him all of your experiences. —Luisita

As the train wound through the landscape north of Guadalajara, Mother Luisita's finger traced the route on the itinerary. They would travel a total of 1,095 miles.

She began to pray, allowing her heart to surrender itself to the Lord anew as each stop brought her farther away from all that she knew and loved. All her life she had known God. To pray was as essential as breathing, eating, or sleeping. She prayed quietly and unobtrusively. She slipped into prayer habitually, and this gentle transition turned her thoughts to her home, her family, the Sisters she had left behind, and the evil that was ready and eager to snatch them all with its iron grasp. She closed her eyes.

Why is this train making so many stops? I have a feeling this isn't going to be a quick journey.

She gazed out the window and couldn't help comparing the bleak panorama with her beautiful Atotonilco, imbued with the fragrance of its lime orchards, lemon flowers, jasmine, and luscious fruit. Atotonilco was known as "the Garden of Jalisco."

The word *jasmine* means "gift from God." Its exquisite white flowers look like stars. Its fragrant aroma is soothing and calming, and Mother Luisita allowed its memory to pour over her as a healing balm, giving rest to her tired soul.

Adelante! Onward!

Her Sisters were like Atotonilco's jasmine flower. They were a healing presence to all, carrying God's love into the dark night of President Calles's godless regime.

One by one, more memories of her childhood in Atotonilco surfaced. They eased her body and spirit, and she felt her tight muscles yielding to the rhythmic motion of the train. She sighed quietly and murmured a prayer as images of her childhood restored her. Thinking about her childhood began to lessen the recurring flashbacks that had been plaguing her—flashbacks of soldiers, gunfire, blood, dead bodies hanging from telephone poles along the railroad tracks, and the diseases that were sweeping through Los Altos as a result of the unclaimed dead bodies spread out stiffly on its cobblestone streets.

She focused on Atotonilco, with its fragrant orange and lemon blossoms and exquisite jasmine and the peace and security of her childhood home.

Yes. This is what I will do while on this train. I'll think about all the good things, the beautiful things that have taken place in my life.

She drifted off to sleep.

Chapter 4

My Atotonilco

How beautiful it is to be in the hands of God, searching
His divine gaze, in readiness to do whatever He wishes.

—Letter to Mother Socorro, 1932

As the train wound its way through the muggy countryside, children's voices awakened Mother Luisita.

"Mama! I'm hungry!"

"Where's the bathroom?"

The voices came from two children a few rows ahead of the Sisters. The little girl looked about three years old, and her brother about six. The boy was kicking the seat in front of him. The girl was pouting, wanting more attention than the parents were able to give her. As Mother Luisita watched the parents try to comfort and quiet the children, the voices of these tired little ones reminded her of her beloved children in her orphanage in Atotonilco.

Margarita María motioned to the parents.

"If you want to send one of your children over to me, I'll play with your little one for a while."

"Thank you, señorita," said the father, and with a relieved smile, he sent his daughter over to spend some time with the gracious lady who offered to help.

IN THE FACE OF DARKNESS

"What's your name?" asked Margarita María.

"Dolores."

"How old are you, Dolores?"

Margarita María held up one finger. Dolores shook her head. She held up two fingers. Dolores shook her head again.

Then shyly, Dolores looked at Margarita María and held up three short, chubby fingers and smiled. A friendship was born. Margarita María began to teach little Dolores some songs with hand motions, and the mom and dad were able to rest awhile.

I miss Atotonilco's children.

Mother Luisita's life and work were devoted to the poor, the sick, and especially those children who had been abandoned or orphaned and left to fend for themselves. The townsfolk came to call Mother Luisita "the Soul of Atotonilco" because over and over they had witnessed her compassionate outpouring of love to the disadvantaged, especially to those living in utter misery.

Mother Luisita had always lived in Atotonilco. She was born there on June 21, 1866, the third child of Epigmenio de la Peña and Luisa Navarro. Her birthday and her mother's were on the feast of Saint Aloysius Gonzaga. Like her mother, she was named after this saint, being called María Luisa, which very soon became Luisita.

Mother Luisita's thoughts turned to Atotonilco, to her formative years. The first thought that came to mind was that evening when she and her father were sitting comfortably in the courtyard of their home and he had spoken to her from his heart. She had received new insights from her father that night and still remembered the conversation, almost word for word.

My Atotonilco

Her father had turned to her and said, "Luisita, God has blessed our family very much. We are responsible for the livelihood of many people. We've acquired more and more property, and now we own many of the estates in Los Altos. Our estates provide employment for our workers, who keep them yielding such abundant harvests. We have many orchards, and with each one specializing in specific fruits or vegetables, we depend on them very much."

That was the first time Luisita began to understand the responsibility of a member of the upper class born into a family of wealthy landowners. This realization was a milestone during her growing-up years, and she still felt its impact. Yes, she understood the words *responsibility* and *stewardship*. That stewardship had brought her on this journey to save the vocations of the Sisters, especially the younger ones, from the moral dangers during these perilous times.

Even now, as Mother Luisita sat in the first-class compartment of the train, she could hear the sounds of the hacienda and feel the warmth of family and friends. She loved nature and felt at home close to the rich soil of their estates. During her childhood, the delicious fragrance of the fertile fields and orchards imprinted themselves upon her heart.

I'm already homesick.

At first glance, Atotonilco el Alto, nestled within the shade of Jalisco's stately mountains, looks like one enormous garden. Amid its fields and flowers, the charming town of Atotonilco is filled with old traditions and joyful harmony. In the de la Peña home, the outpouring of love from her closely knit, staunchly Catholic family was experienced by all who knew them. Although she was Luisa and Epigmenio's third child, she was always the oldest because the first two children had died in infancy. Luisita had never seen her two older sisters, María Magdalena Clotilde del Refugio, who was born on their family's estate of La Labor in 1861, and María Clotilde de Jesus, who was born in Atotonilco in 1864.

Atotonilco was more than a town to Luisita. It was a way of life, a culture unto itself, and she loved being a part of it.

She closed her eyes.

My God within me, I adore You.

She began to say the Rosary, and because she could be seen, she did not use her rosary beads. Instead, she counted each decade on her fingers.

Chapter 5

Agapita

*Be at peace. All of us have difficulties of
some kind or another in this life.*

—Letter to Mother Elena, 1932

"Ouch!"

Mother Luisita's arm hurt. Crossing her arms nonchalantly, she felt the site of her recent inoculation. It was hot.

Infected. Well, it will just have to wait. Can't do anything about it here.

Mother Luisita had entered the world in poor health and had been sickly ever since. As a child, it became second nature for her to take extra rest and spend days at a time indoors when she longed to romp and play in the sunshine. As a toddler, she would go from room to room following the sun's rays that shifted through the various windows. She would play in the sunlit patches, turning toward the sun and allowing its rays to fall upon her. That was the best she could manage when she was too ill to go outside.

Soon it was time for her to begin school. In those days, Atotonilco had no formal school buildings, desks, or chalkboards; classes were given in the teacher's home, where all the basics were learned, as well as art, music, and embroidery and needlepoint for the girls.

Mother Luisita felt a slight tug at her sleeve.

"Talk to me, please," Teresa whispered quietly. A cold, clammy hand landed on top of Mother's hand. Mother turned toward her suddenly.

"What's the matter, Teresa?"

"I'm very frightened."

"What's frightening you?" she asked as if she didn't know.

"I can't think. I can't rest. I almost can't breathe. I can't get the horrible thoughts out of my mind." Her eyes filled with tears.

Mother looked at Teresa. Her breathing was rapid and labored. Taking Teresa's hand, she held it tightly, trying to warm it up.

It is getting to all of us. No wonder. With so little nourishment and forced to hide indoors in those small, cramped rooms. But, most of all, my dearest Lord, we've been denied the consolation of the sacraments.

The cumulative effect from all this takes its toll, and one day the dam breaks.

"Yes, Teresa, I will. I'll talk with you. Just now, I was thinking about my childhood, and how Agapita—I always called her 'Pita'—came to us. Have I ever mentioned her to you?"

"Well, I know that your father asked Agapita to come and live at your home to help take care of you. But, no, I don't know the details. I'd love to hear more about her."

"All right then," Mother Luisita replied. "We'll turn our minds to beauty and goodness, virtue and prayer. All these I learned from my Pita.

"One day, when I was quite young, maybe five years old or so, I heard my mother and father speaking in the garden. They were discussing me. As I listened, I heard them trying to decide whether to keep me in school."

The train was picking up speed now, and the countryside whisked past them.

"Not long after that, my father gave me a governess who would be my private tutor. She was one of his relatives who had never married, Agapita. Teresa, from the first moment I met her, I loved my Pita, and how well I know that she loved me."

Mother Luisita rested her head on the back of her comfortable seat and smiled. Recollections of Pita's love and devotion, and her extraordinary influence on her character, danced across her mind, one after another, like beautiful birds flying one by one in a perfect formation.

Teresa saw Mother Luisita's face soften the moment she began talking about Pita.

"Pita was a holy, prayerful person. She was deeply contemplative, and by working with her and listening to her, and by spending hours and hours with her, I suppose some of it rubbed off on me. You see, she taught me the secret of prayer and shared with me the gift of contemplation. It was from Pita that I learned to penetrate the secrets of God's holy creation.

"I remember how Pita and I would often look up at the stars after the sunset and praise God our Father, Who created them for us. You see, to us the stars were symbols of hope. In our gentle Atotonilco nights, we looked for each magnificent star. Sometimes we would try to count them. That's when Pita would say, 'Imagine, Luisita, our good God created these wondrous stars for you, to give you joy and pleasure.'"

Mother Luisita discreetly glanced at Teresa.

Good. She is breathing easier now, and her fists are no longer clenched.

"Sometimes we would stroll together through the orchard and then have a picnic by the lake, one of our favorite places.

IN THE FACE OF DARKNESS

We would sit on one of the uneven, bumpy benches looking up at the sky and marveling at the beautiful white birds that flew over our heads."

Teresa nodded. "I remember your beautiful property. As a child, I loved going there."

Mother Luisita smiled and continued. "When I close my eyes, I can still hear the wind rushing through my hair and see the trees gently swaying in the breeze. Together, Pita and I soaked in the colors of the different flowers surrounding us. We were completely at peace, contemplating God in our special place."

Teresa smiled and settled back more comfortably against her cushioned headrest. "I like to discover God's footprint in nature, too. I love to pray and meditate on God's creation. So you learned to pray from Pita? Not your parents?"

"Well, of course I learned about God and how to pray from my mother and father: the Sign of the Cross, how to hold a rosary, how to move my fingers along the beads, my morning and bedtime prayers."

Mother Luisita took a moment to think. Then she continued: "When Pita came to live with us, her easy and intimate conversation with God inspired me. Her ability to see Him everywhere opened my eyes to His presence.

"The two of us would watch the seasons come and go. We would check for the first signs of spring and look for birds' nests and sprouting leaves. Pita would tell me that God Himself breathes fresh new life back into His creation. She said that what was dead and brown God replaces with tender, green shoots peeking out of the brown soil.

"Pita and I were always together. Nothing about her was superficial. Her deeply interior soul received the gift of prayer from Our Lord."

Teresa looked up quizzically. "Do you think she was a saint?"

"That's a hard question to answer. Who knows? Only God knows the heart, but I can say that Pita's heart, which I grew to know and love, was very close to God. I'm positive of that.

"I have another story about Pita. Would you like to hear it?"

Teresa nodded.

Chapter 6

Raising Luisita

*The interior soul knows how to work and live and remain
recollected at the same time. Between Jesus and the soul there
flows a current that no one sees and a dialogue that no one hears.*

—From the spiritual notes of Mother Luisita

"Please, I would like to hear your story very much. I need you right now." Teresa stopped and took a slow, deep breath. Then she continued, "I am so afraid. You are giving me something else to think about." Her eyes watered.

"All right then. First of all, did you know that my parents had to resort to strict discipline to help me overcome my stubbornness, arrogance, and pride?"

Teresa's eyes were wide open now. "I find that hard to believe!" Mother Luisita was the kindest, sweetest person she had ever known.

Mother Luisita's mouth formed a wry half smile. Behind it was a lifetime of struggling to overcome her personal character defects. "Ah, Teresa, I understand very well the interior battles that are needed to acquire virtues. Looking back on my youth, I see God's hand in my parents' strong discipline. It prepared me for what God was going to ask of me in the future.

"Looking back now, I realize that my parents took very seriously their obligation to form their children's characters by helping us develop a deep inner strength — the strength that even at this very moment is bringing us, with God's help, through this terrible persecution.

"Also, I wasn't accustomed to playing with other children, as I was alone so often. The twins weren't born until I was nine years old. At first, I didn't want to be near the twins. I didn't even like them. So, one day after they were born, I packed a bag and told my mother I was leaving and going to live with my grandmother because she would appreciate me and give me some attention."

Teresa shook her head. "I find that hard to believe, Mother."

"Well, that's the way I was, Teresa. My parents did take me to visit my grandmother, but they brought me back home that evening, and in time I learned to love and cherish my little sisters.

"I loved to ride my little pony and, later, my magnificent horse. Pita told me that my father would become very upset when he discovered that I was rarely at home anymore. He would go around the house calling my name. He'd ask my mother, Pita, and the servants, 'Where is Luisita?' And the answer was always the same."

The rhythm of the train and the stories of Mother's childhood began to bring Teresa a sense of security and stability, and she was able to forget for a while the horrors that were haunting her.

Mother Luisita continued. "Someone would tell my father, 'I saw her on her horse riding through the haciendas of the valley,' or one of the servants would venture, 'I saw her bridling the horse, getting ready to leave.' My family and friends had told me that I was becoming an accomplished horsewoman, and that flattered me.

"My mother was a very strong woman. She was determined and persistent. She never gave up on me. I don't know if she planned her hard lessons according to a schedule, but all I know is that every so often, she would test me, and let me tell you, her testing was very hard."

"What kind of tests?" asked Teresa, who was by now becoming totally absorbed in her cousin's story.

"I had several harsh awakenings, all provided by my mother, who saw my character defects. When I became an adult, she shared with me that after much prayer, she had decided what she had to do. She set out to humble me, Teresa. It didn't happen every day. She chose special days when I really wanted to go somewhere. And then the axe would fall."

Teresa looked at her quizzically. "What do you mean, the axe would fall? What kinds of things did she do?"

"She sent me to her school of obedience, Teresa, with her custom-tailored lessons on humility. I think that my stubbornness and haughtiness were probably just masks to hide my shyness. My mother saw all this and told me that she was very aware that I had the potential for greatness but that I lacked discipline and humility.

"Sometimes, when there were events that I really wanted to attend, and I was already dressed and ready to go, my mother would take back the permission she had already given me. I would have to stay home at her whim. And I didn't like that! Then, as I sat in my room pouting, my mother would tell me she changed her mind and would give me her permission. So, I'd get myself ready again, only to be told that it would be better if I stayed home.

"This happened over and over, far too many times to count. It was a horrible way to learn, but it worked. I really have no idea how many times it happened — sometimes it would happen on the day of the bullfights, at other times on the day of big fiestas, or on a day of an outing or party with family and friends."

IN THE FACE OF DARKNESS

"How old were you when all this was going on?"

"Ever since I left Miss Reynoso's school. So, most of my childhood. Yes, my mother attacked my vanity, my haughty pride, and my extreme sensitivity. I was often very upset. Under it all, though, and especially now that I'm an adult, I realize that her love was not harsh. It is very true, Teresa, that she taught me with an iron hand, yet she had an open and gentle heart. She brought out the best in me."

Teresa kept shaking her head, her eyes wide in disbelief. "Incredible! I don't know this Luisita you are describing to me."

"My father also had his way of dealing with me. He often rode through the estates, checking on the haciendas and talking with our workers on our ranches. One day, while I was riding with him—I must have been eleven or twelve—he stopped and spoke with some of our workers. It was a beautiful day, and I was wearing one of my favorite dresses. The weather was just right, not too hot and not too cold. A slight breeze fluttered through the trees. I don't know exactly where my mind was when my father called out to me, 'Luisita, would your tongue wear out if you greeted our workers?' Then I realized that I was completely self-absorbed—everything was me, me, me! To tell you the truth, I didn't think about others, including the workers my father wanted me to greet. I was too busy thinking about myself.

"Later, my father told me that he had spoken to me sharply because this wasn't an isolated incident and that he had witnessed my arrogance many times and was tired of it. This was a grace-filled moment for me, because God gave me a glimpse of the haughty, stuck-up child I had become. From that day on, I have tried to live in the moment, fully present to the people near me, regardless of their social class."

"No one sees any haughtiness in you now. Truly."

Raising Luisita

Mother Luisita gently placed her hand on Teresa's.

Good. Her hand is no longer cold.

"I hope you don't mind my asking, but how were you able to change?" Teresa asked.

"Only by God's grace and the hard lessons my mother and father taught me. Does that answer your—"

Brakes screeched. Packages fell. Passengers lurched forward. The engine came to a sudden stop. Mother Luisita paled. Teresa and Margarita María sat paralyzed in their seats. Teresa's lips were moving silently in prayer.

What's going on? Are soldiers attacking the train?

Margarita María murmured the Hail Mary over and over again.

"What's going on?"

Fear descended on all the passengers.

Chapter 7

As Strong as Oaks

Let's rid ourselves of those tinsel-like virtues that shine but at
the least touch fall apart. That type of virtue isn't for religious,
and much less for Carmelites. Our Holy Mother Saint Teresa
taught her daughters to be as strong as oak trees, and not
like straw, which is always knocked down by the wind.

—Letter to Sister Carmen, 1931

"Your attention, please! Your attention, please!"

The conductor's strong voice could be heard over the din. "We have arrived at a collapsed tunnel. Gather all your things. We will walk together to the other train waiting for us. Be sure to bring all your things. Have your claim tickets ready so you can pick up your baggage from our baggage car. Be very careful. It is easy to slip. The ground is still very muddy from the summer monsoons. Watch out for each other and proceed carefully. Please carry your children or hold their hands."

The three Carmelites obediently stood up, reached for their luggage, and waited in line with all the other passengers filling up the narrow aisle. José took Mother Luisita aside and whispered, "I'll walk with you as long as possible. Here, let me show you how to balance your luggage so it will be easier for you to carry. Be vigilant. Support each other. For heaven's sake, don't slip. Look down carefully each time you take a step. I'm going to ask the conductor if this train will wait so I can come along to assist you during your muddy walk."

"Come on, we can do it!" Lorenzo called out to them. "The conductor is right. Be very careful as you walk."

Mother Luisita peeked inside the tunnel. How dark it was! Looking around, she also noticed an embankment on either side of the tunnel. One side of the embankment had collapsed. The other one looked passable.

The larger, heavier baggage was being removed from the baggage car and placed on the soggy ground. Each person had to present a claim ticket to retrieve luggage.

José returned.

"Okay. The train is going to stay right where it is until you are all safely aboard your other train. It won't return to Guadalajara until all of us who are helping passengers come back again."

"I think we should pair up so we can support each other," Lorenzo added. "I'll help Luisita."

Lorenzo gave José an amused look followed by a sideways glance at Margarita María's red high heels.

José laughed. "I'll help Margarita María," he said. "Teresa, are you all right to walk by yourself?"

She nodded.

"Good. Stay close to me."

The conductor's voice rang out. "All right, everyone. Let's begin walking. Take it slowly, please. Watch where you are going."

Lorenzo linked arms with Mother Luisita to steady her as they began their trek to the waiting train. They had walked about fifteen minutes when a man shouted, "Watch out!"

As Strong as Oaks

They looked up quickly. Someone had accidentally dropped a suitcase from the upper ledge of the embankment. It missed Mother Luisita's head by inches. It all happened so fast that no one showed any fear, and it was over within seconds.

Walking was difficult and very slow. After an hour, when all the passengers had reached the waiting train, Lorenzo was amazed to see that he and Mother Luisita made it safely to the train before the younger Margarita María, who needed to take the hike much slower in her high heels.

By the time all the passengers boarded the train, it was already dusk. No one felt like talking. Everyone was exhausted. They were all dirty. Some passengers had caked-on mud up to their knees.

When Margarita María found her seat, she sat down gratefully and breathed a sigh of relief. Her feet hurt a lot. She looked down and, with a wry smile, chuckled to herself when she saw that her fancy shoes were red no longer, but she was too tired to care. Mother Luisita and Teresa, grateful that their tunnel escapade was now finished, tried to relax.

But that was not to be.

As this next stage of their journey began, the three women soon discovered that this replacement train was very different from the one they had traveled in from Guadalajara. It was definitely inferior. When night fell, the entire train remained in the dark. There was no light anywhere. This train had no lights! In the semitropical, blistering June heat, there was no cooling ventilation system of any kind. And they would soon be entering the Sonoran Desert.

As Carmelites, they were used to deprivations and sacrifices. Well, now they would have at least two more. Praise God!

Before long, most of the passengers had eaten a light supper and turned in for the night. After the three Sisters had eaten their supper, Mother Luisita asked them to lean closer to her, and then she spoke in a low voice.

"Our Holy Mother Saint Teresa made many journeys, did she not? We, too, like our Holy Mother, are traveling with many deprivations and hardships. Remember that Saint Teresa taught her daughters to be as strong as oak trees, not like straw, which is always knocked down by the wind.

"It doesn't matter if we are trampled upon, if it becomes a means of raising ourselves closer to God, and once elevated to God, may we remain that way. We have to be strong and valiant with ourselves and not let suffering get the best of us. All pain is transitory, and as our Holy Mother Saint Teresa tells us, any pain that is not eternal is no pain at all."

She searched the faces of the other two Sisters and was satisfied that they understood what she had been saying.

The porter had already prepared their beds for the night. Mother Luisita and Margarita María had lower berths in one section. Teresa was in the bottom berth of the adjoining section.

Although a washroom was available, it wasn't adequate. People did their best to freshen up, but the room was small and poorly supplied.

Two passengers walked into the Sisters' compartment. They had tickets for the upper berths. Mother Luisita and Margarita María detected alcohol on the breath of the two travelers as they hoisted themselves into their berths.

The three Sisters were already in bed when the men in the upper berths began a long night of arguing back and forth. They began in low tones, but before long the decibels began to rise. The Sisters did not see the arguers, but definitely heard them through their privacy curtains. No one said anything. The men in the upper berths proceeded to toss and turn and argue and laugh most of the night.

The individual privacy curtains that the porter put up were made of a thick material that kept the summer heat in. It became one, long, sweltering, loud night for the three refugees.

Teresa, struggling to breathe in the stifling lower berth, took a few minutes to think about their situation as she turned in for the night. It was still June 20. They had boarded their first train at noon in Guadalajara and had reached the collapsed tunnel after traveling only four hours. By the time they reached the waiting train, it was already twilight, and they were not scheduled to arrive in Nogales until midmorning on June 23.

"Oh my goodness, that means we have two more nights and two and a half more days on this train!"

With her mouth firmly set, she whispered to herself, "Well, I can do this. This is nothing. Nothing compared with what we've already been through."

Chapter 8

The Bag She Kept

*Regarding your family, pray for them and expect everything from
our good God, Who loves them more than you do. They are
also His children, and He shed His precious blood for them.*

—Undated letter to Sister María of the Sacred
Heart during the religious persecution

The following morning, as dawn etched its way across the horizon, rays of sunlight pierced through the eastern windows of the train. The three Carmelites were among the first to awaken. They prayed their morning prayers in soft whispers, barely audible. When they went to bed the night before, they were nearing Mazatlán, Sinaloa; now, upon awakening, they were approaching Guaymas in the state of Sonora with its hot desert.

They whispered the psalms of the Little Office of the Blessed Virgin.

For a day in Your courts is better than a thousand
outside.
I would rather stand at the threshold of the house of
my God
than dwell in the tents of wickedness.

IN THE FACE OF DARKNESS

For the Lord God is a sun and shield
The Lord gives grace and glory;
No good thing does He withhold from those who
    walk uprightly.

O Lord of hosts,
How blessed are those who trust in You!

Praying the familiar verses brought them comfort, and they relaxed a little. They meditated. They ate breakfast and quietly wished Luisita a happy sixty-first birthday.

This is certainly one birthday I won't forget!

There wasn't much to do on the train. They read a little. They prayed awhile. From time to time, they dozed off. Margarita María got tired of just sitting. So she stood up, stretched her legs discreetly, and walked a short distance back and forth several times. Then she sat down again and turned to Mother Luisita.

"May I talk with you awhile, Auntie?" using the name they had called Mother Luisita since the persecution began.

"Of course."

"I saw a table toward the front. Shall we go up and sit there? It will give you a little exercise."

Shaking her head, Mother answered, "If you don't mind, I'd rather not draw attention to us. Ask me here."

Margarita María's lips quivered. "Mother, do you think we'll ever go back to Mexico?"

"I think so. I hope so. We are all in God's hands. He knows what is best and will allow to happen only what is best for us. I firmly believe that and hold on to it with all my might."

"It's just that I'm already homesick."

"I know. So am I."

They grew silent. Mother Luisita recalled something

Archbishop Pedro Loza slapped me on the cheek when I was confirmed. Pita said that the slap was a symbol of the hardships that Christians would face in their Christian lives. Ah, my Pita, you told me that Confirmation gave me the grace I would need to overcome hardships and persecutions.

I never dreamt that I would call upon that grace as much as I have lately.

Lord, stir up within us all the strengthening graces of our Confirmation. We really need Your strength right now, right here.

Mother Luisita gently picked up the leather bag she had brought with her. She had carried the bag with her ever since 1896, when her husband, Doctor Pascual Rojas, had died. It was the bag he used on his many house calls to the sick people of Atotonilco.

They had spent fourteen happy years together, from their wedding day in 1882 until Pascual's death in 1896. After he died, Luisita kept his bag, and it had traveled with her these many years, accompanying her to countless hiding places, sometimes in a different house each night. It now carried the precious correspondence that was her link with her Sisters hiding throughout Guadalajara and its suburbs. This practical bag, which had brought healing to the sick, evoked memories of Pascual and their devoted service together to the poor of Atotonilco. Those were good years.

Luisita recalled that day when she was only eight or nine and Doctor Rojas had come by to visit with her father and she had remarked to her mother, "I wonder who is going to marry Doctor Rojas."

Many years later, as it turned out, she was the one.

IN THE FACE OF DARKNESS

∞

A year later, one of her relatives told her that she had overheard her father remark, "Our Luisita is different now. I find myself changed when I am with her, compelled to respect her."

Fourteen-year-old Luisita knew she had changed. She felt it. Her soul was maturing. Her interior life of prayer was deepening. Through God's grace, her parents' guidance, and the companionship of Pita, she was transformed into a kind, cultured, beautiful young woman.

Festivals and evening concerts took place in the city's principal garden, located in the plaza directly across from their spacious home. Her family would open the front doors in order to appreciate the music and enjoy the summer evening. People didn't understand why Luisita, who loved music so much, would drift off into her own thoughts so often during their summer concerts.

Sometimes one of her friends would tease her. "Listen, Luisita, we are being serenaded! Don't you like music anymore?"

"Ah, yes," she answered, and then she would close her eyes again in prayer. A friend standing nearby heard her whisper, "My God, give me a holy heart with a pure intention to please You" as she closed her eyes again.

Along with her love for music, there was something else, something stirring within her soul that she did not understand. That night, she wanted to think and pray about it, but the blaring instruments and the worldly music distracted her. During her hours of communion with God, she had begun to feel within herself the nudging of the Holy Spirit to follow another path, difficult and far away — the consecrated life of a religious Sister. She had also begun to realize that whenever Doctor Rojas would visit her father, they would end up talking about her.

Her parents had noticed a transformation in their oldest daughter. She was no longer the arrogant, stubborn Luisita. She had matured not only physically but spiritually as well. Her parents had begun to realize the profound depths of their daughter's soul.

When it was time for her to marry, they knew that she would need a husband with the same depth of character that she had. Pascual Rojas, who had been designated as her future spouse many years ago, was just such a person.

Luisita was shy and demure. Pascual was optimistic and outgoing. Luisita preferred quiet, and Pascual loved excitement. She was only fifteen and he was thirty when they were married in a traditional arranged marriage, as was the custom in Atotonilco.

Following Pascual's death, fourteen years later, the only things that Luisita kept from the marriage were the crucifix her husband had given her as a gift and the statue of Saint Pascual, his patron saint, kneeling in adoration before the Blessed Sacrament. Later, she asked that his doctor bag be sent to her as well.

As she sat in the stifling, muggy train, Luisita found that looking at the bag somehow brought calmness. It was as if she were holding not a mere bag but cherished memories of her wonderful life with Pascual. She recalled the midmorning sunlight that had poured in through the large church windows as they walked up the aisle on their wedding day; the exquisite white flowers that had adorned the altar; the music, performed by a complete orchestra; the trumpets and kettle drums during the wedding march.

The couple enjoyed a long, leisurely honeymoon, getting to know each other as they traveled between towns. They were amazed to learn how alike their interests were as they enjoyed the art galleries and concerts in Mexico City and the quaint little towns along the way. They discovered the depth of their mutual desire to be of service to the poor.

Mother Luisita looked again at the bag and smiled as she recalled asking her husband if they could visit some convents during their honeymoon. During their stop at the Conceptionist convent in Morelia, basking in the aura of that holy place, she had felt drawn to remain there with the Sisters. She didn't ever want to leave that holy place. When the superior discovered that Pascual was her husband, she very kindly told Luisita to go home with him, and perhaps at some future time, she could return. She recalled that Pascual took her arm, saying, "Luisita, come with me now, and someday you will return."

She realized once again how kind both the superior and Pascual had been as they had taken into account her naiveté and her young age and, thanks be to God, had understood her request and then had helped her to move on.

Our Lord had not blessed their marriage with children, despite their making so many novenas, and Pascual had told her one day, "Luisita, since Our Lord has willed not to give us a family, the poor shall be our children."

From that moment on, they had dedicated themselves and invested everything — time and fortunes — to help the poor and the sick. It had been their mission, and it had brought them even closer together. Luisita had learned so much from Pascual about taking care of the sick.

Mother Luisita looked at Margarita María and smiled.

"Mother, you seemed so very far away just now. Were you praying?" Margarita María asked.

"Yes. Both reminiscing and praying. Now, try to rest awhile. That's what I'm going to do. Margarita María, may God Our Lord give you peace of soul."

The Bag She Kept

∞

The train absorbed the Sonoran Desert's sweltering heat on this final leg of the journey. The air in their compartment was stagnant and filled with a variety of odors. The Sisters offered up their discomfort for their suffering Mexico.

The lack of light at night and the lowered oxygen level from the poor ventilation made the two and a half days and three nights very long indeed. In addition, sleep was almost impossible because of the noise from their neighbors on the top berths. They all felt lethargic and at times even weak. From working many years alongside her husband, Mother Luisita noticed the classic symptoms of lack of oxygen among the three of them. Each of them had dry skin, headaches, itchy eyes, and dry throats. It was obvious that they weren't taking in enough good air.

During those two and a half days, other passengers spent extended time in the dining car or the lounge car. It was then that Mother Luisita shared with the other Sisters various topics of Carmelite spirituality and read to them from the writings of Saint Teresa of Avila.

"Oh, my daughters, how ardently I want you to be true religious with solid virtues. We all know that we will be leaving our beloved Mexico as we enter the United States. I'd like you to think about the words of our Holy Mother Saint Teresa during our last few hours on this train: 'Let nothing disturb you. Let nothing frighten you.' I know that our future is uncertain and that we all have so many unanswered questions filling our hearts. Let's all live those words of our Holy Mother Saint Teresa of Jesus as we cross the border soon. Nothing happens without Our Lord permitting it.

"So, let us place all in God's hands. He knows what is best for us. God our Father in His unfathomable goodness and mercy will provide everything we need. Just you wait and see!" And the peace that surpasses all understanding fell upon the three refugees in that aged train chugging its way slowly to a country of religious freedom.

Chapter 9

In His Hands

Suffer and wait.
Pray and expect.

— From the spiritual notes of Mother Luisita

Before leaving Guadalajara, Mother Luisita had heard several versions of what took place at the border during the immigration processing.[8] She didn't know which one to believe, so she

---

[8] "Before the early 1900s, Mexicans were able to move freely across the border without regulation. With the Mexican Revolution, American officials had an increased awareness of the open border, and Mexican immigrants were categorized as diseased and dirty. Mexicans were bathed every time they crossed the border. At the border, entrants were stripped naked, showered with kerosene, examined for lice and nits, and vaccinated against smallpox. This policy lasted into the 1920s. In 1917, an inspection and quarantine was issued based on a threat of typhus. The threat lasted several months, but the medical inspection continued into the 1930s, even after there was no longer a serious threat. Medical inspection of Mexican immigrants was not opposed because health was a prerequisite for labor. The inspections were also differentiated by class, as a sizeable number of Mexicans — especially recognized commuters, those who were well dressed, and those who rode first-class

decided to keep the worrisome stories to herself and not burden the others with some of the alarming details she had been told.

One thing she did know: every version of what happened at the border had one common statement—the processing protocol was not as embarrassing and upsetting if you were traveling first-class.

About noon on June 23, 1927, the train reached Nogales, the border town between Mexico and the United States. The Southern Pacific Railroad had two depots there: one on the Mexican side of the border and one on the American side, in Nogales, Arizona.

Passengers hastily gathered their belongings and began leaving the train. This was a new experience for most of them. An undercurrent of anxiety ran through the passengers as they wondered if everything they brought with them was correct, or if any unforeseen obstacle might turn them back after having come so far.

The first-class passengers were escorted off the train first. The other passengers disembarked next. Mother Luisita watched them as they were directed another way.

I wonder where all those other passengers are going?

As the Sisters walked to the American side, Ignacio De la Torre, who was a good friend of Archbishop Francisco Orozco y Jiménez, and his wife, María, and one of their sons met them at the United States depot.[9] Their assistance greatly helped the

---

on the train—were exempt from the disinfection drill." Howard Markel and Alexandra Minna Stern, "The Foreignness of Germs: The Persistent Association of Immigrants and Disease in American Society" *Milbank Quarterly* 80, no. 4 (January 2002): 757–788, doi:10.1111/1468-0009.00030.

[9] During the decades when the Cristiada was neither taught nor discussed, the De la Torre family safeguarded numerous

Sisters to figure out what to do next because Ignacio was familiar with the process. First, he took them to the Department of Immigration, where the necessary documents were presented to the authorities.

As soon as they had cleared immigration, Ignacio said, "Sisters, there will be a fairly long wait for the train. My wife would like you to come to our home and rest awhile, and then we would like to take you to lunch at a nearby restaurant before you continue on your journey. I hope you will accept our hospitality."

Later, at the De la Torre home, Mrs. De la Torre said, "Sisters, you'll find soap and other toiletries in the bathroom. And take your time. We have hours before your next train leaves."

Mother Luisita was the first to take her up on her kind offer.

It was here in the De la Torre home that Mother Luisita saw how far the infection in her arm was spreading. An ugly abscess was festering. She could hardly move her arm now, and it was becoming harder and harder for her to keep the wound a secret from her Sisters. After taking a hot bath and placing her lay clothes in the hamper, Mother Luisita put on her habit slowly, piece by piece, while saying the required prayers. Now, she felt ready to board the American train.

One by one, the weary travelers entered the bathroom and then emerged as Carmelite Sisters, smiles on their faces and a spring in their step.

---

invaluable materials from the persecution and the resistance movement. These items are now housed at the University of Arizona. Jean Meyer, *The Cristiada: The Mexican People's War for Religious Liberty* (New York: Square One Publishers, 2013), 87–191.

IN THE FACE OF DARKNESS

When I reach Los Angeles, I'll ask Ramón if he knows a doctor who can take care of this abscess. Thanks be to God I've made it this far, but it will need to be taken care of as soon as possible.

Ramón, the husband of her youngest sister Lupita, was going to meet them at the Los Angeles train station. Also a refugee, he had been in the city for several months.

Ignacio and María treated the Sisters to a good lunch at a nearby restaurant. This was the beginning of a friendship between the De la Torre family and the Carmelite Sisters. The couple generously offered to meet and assist any Carmelite Sister who would enter or leave the United States from that day forward.

Thank You, my Lord, for sending us these good people to take care of all of us at the border. Thank you for Your mercy, Your providence, and Your abounding goodness. I am at peace. I am safe in Your hands.

After lunch, Ignacio accompanied them back to the depot and boarded the train with them to help them locate their reserved seats. Then he left them. A few minutes later, they heard the now familiar train whistle followed by the conductor on the platform calling out, "All aboard!"

The train began to move slowly, and as it picked up speed, Mother Luisita knelt down in the aisle. The other two women soon joined her, and together they prayed aloud the Te Deum, the most ancient prayer of thanksgiving of the Catholic Church. The small group continued praying until they realized that they were blocking the passageway. Calmly getting up, they returned to their seats, reopened their Little Office of the Blessed Virgin Mary, and continued their prayers.

Several people approached them with questions during this final phase of their trip.

"Good evening, Sisters. What order do you belong to?"

"Are you Franciscans? The Franciscan Sisters taught me."

"Sisters, would you please pray for my family? We need lots of prayers right now."

Mother Luisita just watched. She wanted so much to speak with these dear people, to answer their questions and get to know them a little better. She longed to be of service to each of them in any way possible, but she knew absolutely no English. When people tried to speak to her, she could only smile a little and blush.

How frustrating it is for me not to understand. What a heavy cross this will be for me to carry!

And Mother Luisita experienced the first of many headaches as she tried to listen and understand something of Sister Margarita María's conversations in English. Not knowing what else to do, she picked up the route itinerary and browsed through it: Nogales to Tucson — 67 miles; Tucson to Yuma — 240 miles; Yuma to Los Angeles — 270 miles.

She turned to the other two Sisters. With her beautiful smile slowly spreading across her face, she quietly whispered, "We are in the United States. We made it!"

They were free.

Mother Luisita remained deep in thought.

We have a serious obligation to fulfill — to establish a safe haven in the United States. More of our Sisters will be making this journey to freedom. The three of us will prepare the way. And in the future months when other Sisters arrive, everything will be ready for them.

These thoughts gave her peace.

The other Carmelites were also quiet and reflective. They passed through the outer perimeter of the desert and continued into California. The scenery changed again as the train wove in and out of the cities and towns in Southern California.

Despite feeling tired and uncomfortable and not knowing what awaited them or whether they would be successful in the United States, the three refugees exuded a serene confidence. The Holy Spirit's gift of fortitude gave them the vigor and strength their mission required.

Mother Luisita leaned over again and whispered, "*Adelante!* Let us go forward!"

Chapter 10

City of Angels

May Divine Love consume your soul! After all,
that is the reason why we are in the world. All
of the rest is nothing but a puff of smoke!

—Letter to Mother Margarita María, 1930

Around noon on Friday, June 24, 1927, the solemnity of the Sacred Heart of Jesus, three weary Carmelite Sisters arrived at Los Angeles's Central Station, Southern Pacific Railroad's main passenger terminal. The station was an impressive white stucco building with steel, umbrella-style train sheds that could accommodate up to sixteen trains at a time. Built in 1915, the station featured carpeted lounges, a restaurant, a lunch counter, and an emergency hospital.

Ramón Ugarte was waiting for the Carmelites at the station. Their greetings were short and intense. "Sisters, I know how tired you must be! Let's get you home."

Mother Luisita spoke. "Ramón, is it possible for me to see a doctor soon? I need some medical treatment for the smallpox inoculation I received when I got my passport." She tried to downplay the infection as much as possible.

"Yes. Let's go right away," Ramón responded. That's how a visit to the hospital became the first thing they did after stepping off the train.

While she awaited her turn to be seen by the doctor, Mother Luisita spoke with Ramón. He looked well. The last time she had seen him was in Los Altos, and he had been stressed and anxious. The soldiers had been doggedly searching for Ramón. Nothing less than his life was at stake, perhaps even more than hers. He had fled the country quietly and stealthily and managed to send word back to his family that he was safely in the United States.

Ramón spoke softly. "I'm hoping to bring my family to the United States in three months. God willing, they will also travel the new Southern Pacific through line from Guadalajara to Nogales. Pray for them, Mother."

Mother Luisita nodded. She was already thinking ahead.

September would be the perfect time for more Sisters to leave Mexico. It would give us three full months to find a place to live, to get work done, and to learn how to live in this different culture. It feels good to be able to plan something. Looking ahead with some set goals energizes me.

"Ramón, do you think we could bring some more Sisters here on the same train with Lupita and the children?" He stopped and looked at her. Her face was flushed with the fever from her spreading infection, and she was visibly tired. Her pain was apparent, even though she struggled to hide it — the infection in her arm was much worse than she had shared with the others.

"Yes, that is a very good idea! Let's talk about it after you rest for a few days."

He turned to address all three women at the same time. "Sisters, I'm taking you to a rooming house that is a shelter for Mexican refugees. It is certainly not luxurious, but it's affordable.

It's on the corner of Georgia and Eighteenth Streets, near the business section of Los Angeles. You will notice right away that there are several other refugees from Mexico living there. Some of them are priests. You'll probably stay there only a few days and then move along to another place. We need to speak to the bishop to find out where you will be living while you are here in the United States."

The Sisters nodded, grateful that plans had been made ahead of their arrival.

"Luisa Peña," a nurse called from the hallway. Mother Luisita got up and walked over to the nurse. As she and Sister Teresa went down the corridor to the examination room, Ramón, who knew some English, and Sister Margarita María, with her limited English, worked together to fill out the necessary paperwork.

When the doctor finished the procedure, he accompanied her to the waiting room. The nurse spoke to Ramón and Sister Margarita María in English, "She has an abscess. Make sure that she sees a doctor within a week to confirm that the infection is controlled and that there are no further complications."

Ramón and Sister Margarita María translated the request for Mother Luisita, who nodded her assent. Then Ramón turned back to the doctor. "Yes, we'll get it checked out. Thank you very much, doctor. We really needed your services today, and we are very grateful."

As they left the building, the Sisters felt dwarfed by the tall Los Angeles buildings. They were far from their seemingly endless Atotonilco sky, so clear and beautiful. Mother Luisita remained deep in thought.

These three refugees, who appeared somewhat frail and malnourished, were stronger than they looked. Each of the women was a trained spiritual athlete. Passersby saw only serenity and peace on their faces. They had no idea where the Sisters had come from, what they had gone through, or how great was the spiritual strength within their frail bodies.

As for the Sisters, they could tangibly feel the acceptance from the American people—on the train, at the station, at the hospital, and now walking down the sidewalk. Men tipped their hats. People smiled and greeted them with, "Good afternoon, Sisters," as they passed by. A few crossed themselves.

They were in the United States.

Chapter 11

A Solitary Tear

*My God, I love you! This sentence expresses all the
desires of the heart given totally to God, for whom God
is everything and to whom God alone suffices!*

—From the spiritual notes of Mother Luisita

The boardinghouse faced three churches, one on each of the
other corners.

"Look! Three churches and they are all so near where we will
be staying!" said Sister Margarita María excitedly.

"What are their names, Ramón? Why are they so close to
each other?" asked Sister Teresa.

"May we make a visit to the Blessed Sacrament right now?
I would like that very, very much!" Mother Luisita looked up
with expectant eyes.

He merely shrugged his shoulders. "Well, sorry to disappoint
you all, but you see these three churches? Not one of them is
a Catholic Church. Our church, the one where we will attend
Mass tomorrow, is several blocks from here."

The Sisters had never seen so many denominations in one
place. Sister Margarita María exclaimed, "Ramón, what a different

kind of place this City of Angels is! Three churches, and not one of them Catholic—I've never heard of such a thing!"

A familiar aroma greeted the Sisters the moment they entered the boardinghouse—chili! A dish with savory, spicy chili peppers was being prepared in the nearby kitchen.

They looked around the living room, hesitatingly at first. Children were playing. Women were conversing—and in Spanish! They began to feel at home.

The next morning, before dawn, the Carmelites quietly got up. They put on their brown Carmelite habits and prayed the required prayers that went with each part of the habit. First, the soft white coif head covering:

> O my Lord, grant me the grace to prefer death rather than soil my soul by sin. Purify it in Your Precious Blood, and give me perfect contrition for my sin.

Then the coarse brown tunic:

> Clothe me, O my God, with the holy religious habit that I may appear before You in such a manner as my holy habit requires.

Next, the black leather cincture with attached rosary.

> Unite me interiorly to Yourself, O Lord, and attach me to Your goodness by the bonds of charity that can never be broken.

Then the simple brown scapular.

> O my God, grant me the grace to carry with joy and love Your sweet yoke and burden all the days of my life.

And finally, the flowing black veil.

This veil teaches me that I ought to die to the world and to myself in order to live entirely for You.

They felt like themselves again.

No one else was up yet as the women prayed quietly and waited for Ramón to take them to Mass. It was good just to be, relishing the birds' chirping outside their windows and contemplating the pure beauty of the first rays of dawn.

A little after daybreak, Ramón arrived to accompany them to Mass. As they reached the church steps, the three refugees stopped and looked at each other. No words were needed as each Sister savored this moment when they were free to enter, free to attend Mass and receive the sacraments. Before entering the church, they put on their white mantles and silently prayed the accompanying prayer.

O spotless Lamb of God, clothe my soul with the purity and whiteness of those who follow You.

The Mass seemed far too short. After so many months without the consolation of the sacraments, it took discipline and effort to stand up when Ramón whispered gently, "Mother, it's time to leave now. They've prepared breakfast for us at the boardinghouse."

Walking back to the boardinghouse, Ramón added, "Mother, after breakfast, I'll take you to the chancery office in Los Angeles to meet Bishop John Cantwell. Although we have no appointment, I'm sure the bishop will see you, given the circumstances. It is not very far from here."[10]

---

[10] The chancery office is the branch of administration that handles all written documents used in the official government of a diocese.

IN THE FACE OF DARKNESS

∞

A few hours later, the group was on its way to the chancery office. The four entered the building and waited while Ramón spoke with the receptionist. As soon as Bishop Cantwell learned of the three Carmelite refugees waiting to see him, he asked that they be brought right away to his private office.

Conversation with the bishop was almost impossible. Sister Margarita María's English fell woefully short. As they were trying to communicate, Father Leroy Callahan walked by, and Bishop Cantwell called him in to translate. Father Callahan, pastor of San Antonio de Padua Church in East Los Angeles, spoke fluent Spanish. The bishop had asked him months ago to implement a new parish program that would offer spiritual comfort to the Mexican immigrants and contribute to their faith formation.

The bishop had also asked him to accept the position of director of the Confraternity of Christian Doctrine and begin a new bilingual, English and Spanish, catechetical program. In addition, because he spoke seven languages, he was asked to help the Mexican refugees who were pouring into Los Angeles.

"Father, would you translate for me?" the bishop asked him. "These dear Carmelite Sisters have just arrived, refugees from the persecution in Mexico. Would you find out for me what they need and how they would like us to help them?"

Father Callahan, a tall, young priest with a dignified, stately bearing, looked into one of the sweetest faces he had ever seen. Even with the evident stress and tiredness, a beautiful peace emanated from her kind eyes.

He was impressed.

He translated the bishop's question, and Mother Luisita answered calmly.

"Father, please ask the bishop if he could help us find a place in Los Angeles that would be a temporary refuge for our Sisters suffering religious persecution in Mexico."

She slowly turned her glance from his face to Bishop Cantwell's, her calm, steady eyes overriding her fatigue. "Let him know also," she continued as she looked directly at the bishop, "that we would like to work in some capacity for him while we are here in the Diocese of Los Angeles."

As she spoke, a solitary tear fell down Mother Luisita's face.

"What's the matter, Mother?" asked Father Callahan. "You can tell me about it." Because he had worked with so many immigrants, he wanted her to begin the emotional release that all refugees need.

She took a deep breath.

"Father ..." She hesitated.

"Go ahead, Mother, I'm listening." He moved his chair directly across from hers and sat down, waiting.

"Father, the situation in Mexico has become too much to bear. Unimaginable. Unrepeatable ... Guns. Hunger ... Hiding ..." She trembled. "Hiding ..." And for the next ten minutes, she spoke in general terms of the need for her Sisters to find a temporary refuge in the United States.

Father Callahan was deeply moved. He had heard about the religious persecution in Mexico many times. The cloistered Carmelite nuns from Guadalajara had also fled recently to Los Angeles, and the Immaculate Heart Sisters were housing them at their convent in Hollywood. Tens of thousands of Mexicans had already relocated to the City of Angels.

When Mother Luisita finished speaking, Father Callahan turned his eyes toward the bishop. An unspoken compassion passed between them.

"What is she saying, Father?"

Father Callahan told the bishop what Mother Luisita had said and added that Sister Gertrude, superior of the Immaculate Heart Sisters, could possibly offer them hospitality at their convent on Green Avenue. The bishop agreed, and Father Callahan telephoned Sister Gertrude.

"Hello, Sister Gertrude, this is Father Callahan. I have three Carmelite Sisters here with me in the bishop's office. Is there any possibility that you could accommodate three more exiled Mexican Carmelites for a short time until I find more permanent lodging for them? They came in by train yesterday and are very tired. You can imagine their situation."

"Of course, we would be honored to accept them here," Sister Gertrude replied. "We have ample room, and they may stay as long as they need to. Let's see. Today is Saturday. Would it be convenient for you to bring them on Monday, June 27?"

"Perfect. I will see you Monday morning between ten and noon. Thank you very much."

"Father, please let them know in our name that their Immaculate Heart Sisters welcome them now with open arms. Tell them for us, 'Mi casa es su casa.' [My home is your home]."

After Father Callahan hung up the phone, he relayed Sister Gertrude's acceptance to the bishop and then to the Carmelites. A beautiful smile slowly lit up Mother Luisita's face. She looked up gratefully and softly replied, "May God reward you, Father Callahan. May I suggest something? I've been thinking about what we could do to be of service to the bishop. Would he be favorable to my working with the many Mexican refugees here? We know the language and the culture. What does Bishop Cantwell think of this?"

He interpreted the request to Bishop Cantwell.

"Tell her my answer is definitely yes," replied the bishop. "We have a pressing need for this type of ministry. Let her know also that it will be a fruitful apostolate for them."

As they left the bishop's office, Father Callahan drew Mother Luisita aside.

"Mother, I would like to learn more about you and your community. I'll come by the boardinghouse at about ten on Monday morning and take you all to the Immaculate Heart convent. Have your things ready.

"As for now, the first thing is to move you to the Green Avenue convent. It's next to the construction site of our new, magnificent Immaculate Conception Church. You will feel at home there, Mother. The convent has a beautiful chapel. Know for certain that I will be working on your behalf to find the place where you and your Sisters will live. You can't remain here indefinitely with these good Sisters."

The good Lord was moving quickly, putting into motion everything that needed to happen so that they could begin to prepare for the others who would be coming soon. Mother Luisita's thoughts remained focused on everyone they had left behind in Mexico.

Ramón, who had remained in the lobby while the Sisters spoke with Father Callahan and the bishop, stood up and walked toward them as they came into view. Father Callahan extended his hand to Mother Luisita's brother-in-law.

Mother Luisita spoke first. "Father, may I introduce my brother-in-law, Ramón Ugarte?"

Speaking in Spanish, Father Callahan said, "Ramón, I'm pleased to meet you. We've found a place for these dear Sisters to live temporarily until I find more permanent lodging. Between the two of us let's make sure they get everything they need. Feel free to contact me at any time if you or any of the Sisters need me."

He wrote his telephone number on a piece of paper and handed it to Ramón.

After saying good-bye, Ramón and the three refugees left the chancery office and returned to the boardinghouse.

"Ramón, do you have a few minutes for me right now?" asked Mother Luisita. "I'd like to speak with you about something."

A few minutes later they were engrossed in conversation, speaking about a possible September arrival of more Sisters on the train that his wife and children would take.

"Mother, we will need to prepare for the Sisters you would like to come here in the next group. How many are you thinking of?"

"Five for this next group is a good number, Ramón."

"It will be a whole lot easier if they can travel first-class as you three did, don't you think?"

"Yes. Ramón, I'll do my best. I think of them day and night. I won't rest until they are safe in the United States."

The two sat in silence reflecting on the day's events.

"Ramón, thank you again. May God reward you for all that you are doing for us. Let us continue to leave to our good Lord His part, and He will dispose of everything to our greatest advantage. Let us be submissive with true joy and fulfill His most holy will. Either in abundance or in poverty, He will take care that we don't die hungry, and He will give us the things that are necessary because He loves us and is most powerful."

Chapter 12

This Intense Longing

How beautiful it is — the complete submission to the Divine Will.
What a great joy one experiences in saying "the Will of God!"

—Letter to Sister Margarita María, 1930

Father Callahan rang the doorbell of the boardinghouse promptly at ten on Monday morning, wiping his brow with his handkerchief in an attempt to fend off the June humidity. Ramón opened the door and saw the Sisters' sparse luggage stacked neatly in the corner. The three Sisters were there also. Each picked up a piece of luggage and walked to the car.

As they traveled slowly through the midmorning traffic, suddenly Mother Luisita exclaimed, "Oh, no! Not here too!"

With the same eagle eyes that had discovered children living alone in dark caves outside Atotonilco, she now spotted, almost hidden from view, a lone man sitting on his chair of piled-up wooden crates with his dog lying at his feet. Behind him stood his small shelter, constructed of a mishmash of cardboard, tarp, and rope and just large enough for a man and his dog.

As the car stopped at the traffic light, Mother Luisita turned to the Sisters in the backseat and said softly, "Sister Margarita María, we have nothing to give him."

"Who, Mother?"

"The man across the street."

She glanced out the windows. "What man? I don't see him. Where is he?"

"Near the end of the block, under his cardboard house."

So, even in the United States there are people who are homeless, living in meager, cardboard shelters. Of course, I knew that, but it surprised me nonetheless. Thank You, Heavenly Father, for revealing to me that there is work for us here in California.

After a few minutes had passed, the three Sisters noticed a huge building that appeared to be nearing the final phase of its construction. "Father, is that huge building under construction the site of the new church you told us about on Saturday?" Mother Luisita asked.

"Yes, Sisters, that is exactly where you are going. You are looking at the almost-finished, beautiful Immaculate Conception Church. The convent is behind it. This parish was established almost twenty years ago."

As they came closer to the school building, they heard the carefree laughter of children.

Suddenly, Sister Margarita María's eyes lit up.

"Listen, everyone! Look, there they are!" Her eyes danced.

School uniforms. Playground games. Sisters dressed in blue habits supervising the playground. They couldn't take in enough of these familiar sights and sounds. Children of different ages were playing together. Some were engrossed in a robust game of dodgeball. Others were jumping rope. Some were singing while they played.

"Look, we are back with children again. Father, did I tell you that some of us are teachers and that we taught in our schools before the persecution?"

Then Mother Luisita turned to Father Callahan and sighed softly. "But now we are forced to teach in secret groups in private homes and even out in the orchards. Our schools have been closed for almost a year."

When they arrived at the front porch of the convent, they rang the doorbell. Sister Gertrude answered the door herself.

"Good morning, Father. It is good to see you again. Welcome, dear Sisters, welcome to Los Angeles, the City of Angels, under the patronage of Our Lady of the Angels." She embraced each Carmelite and directed the three refugees to follow her straight into their beautiful convent chapel.

Each Sister knelt as close to the tabernacle as possible and prayed silently, taking in the chapel's prayerful stillness and savoring the hint of incense still lingering in the air.

Sister Gertrude tiptoed into the chapel and whispered, "Some of our Sisters are here to greet you," pointing to the doorway behind her. "Others are still over at the school, but they will be with us during lunch. Please step into the hallway with me where they are waiting to welcome you all."

They didn't understand, so Sister Gertrude reduced it to one word that Sister Margarita María understood: "Come."

Sister Margarita María got up and told the others to follow her.

Each Carmelite received a big embrace and a smile. The warm welcome was accompanied by a respectful silence honoring these refugees who had just come from a religious persecution the likes of which they could only imagine. It didn't go unnoticed how worn-out and utterly spent the three Carmelites looked.

Mother Luisita accepted their invitation for the two communities to have their first meal together. They moved into the spacious dining room with its beautiful, dark mahogany table, matching chairs, and highly polished buffet.

IN THE FACE OF DARKNESS

Thanks be to God that some of the Immaculate Heart Sisters spoke Spanish! These generous Sisters had come from their motherhouse in Spain years before. When lunch was over, Sister Gertrude ushered the three refugees into the parlor.

"Mother and Sisters, you have the rest of the day to pray, to rest, whatever you need to recover, and later, if you would like, I can begin teaching you English," Sister Gertrude said.

Sister Margarita María translated.

Sister Gertrude noticed their worn habits. "Do you need any clothing or medication? I'll show you where my office is and demonstrate how to use our washing machine and where we hang our clothing to dry. Oh, and I'll show you where we keep the flatiron and the ironing board."

Again, Sister Margarita María translated.

As a second thought entered Sister Gertrude's mind, she turned and asked a simple question: "Sisters, what you are wearing right now — is that all the clothing you brought with you?"

After her question was translated, the three Carmelites nodded at the same time.

"Oh, I see! Well, at least we know now where to begin, don't we? I'll see what I can do."

Because each Sister had only one habit, they devised a system. Each Sister would wash another Sister's habit while she was resting. It took several hours, but later that afternoon, they felt clean again.

A pile of clothing and toiletries soon appeared in each room, with a promise of more to come. Later that afternoon, Mother Luisita and Sister Margarita María made their way to Sister Gertrude's office. While her clothes were being washed, Sister Margarita María had made good use of the Spanish-English dictionary that the superior had given her that morning. She pored over the words so that she would speak correctly when she met with Sister Gertrude. A small piece of paper contained her handwritten English words expressing their gratitude to Sister Gertrude.

They knocked on the superior's door.

"Please come in," Sister Gertrude said.

Sister Margarita María took out the paper and read slowly the words she had so painstakingly written: "Sister Gertrude, may God reward you for all the clothing and other items you have so charitably given to us and know that He will reward your generosity. May God reward you also for your kind offer to teach us some English."

Sister Margarita María spoke for all of them. She looked down at her paper again and continued, "It's absolutely vital that we learn English as quickly as we can."

Sister Gertrude smiled. After all, she was a teacher herself and realized that much hard work had gone into that beautifully worded and labor-intensive thank-you.

In the afternoon, Father Callahan came by for the first of several chats with Mother Luisita.

"Mother, I need to find out more about your community and its needs. I would like to come by a few days this week and spend about thirty minutes with you each day before I arrange for your extended stay in Los Angeles. Is that agreeable with you?"

"Yes, Father, I would like that very much." He was both authentic and practical, traits that she appreciated.

Father Callahan then posed the question he knew he must ask. Sitting across from her, he folded his hands on the table and gently asked, "Mother, please tell me what you have been through. Tell me about your hopes and dreams regarding coming to our diocese. I would also like to know what you need."

His sincere interest, together with his kind, tactful approach, touched Mother Luisita greatly, and she felt a wave of relief sweep over her. She had someone to talk to, to confide in, and to work with—someone who understood—and that meant the world to her.

Taking a deep breath, she began. "Father, you ask me to share something about the atrocities occurring in Mexico right now, some of which are sacrilegious. You see, we've just come out of chaos, out of mayhem. Everything was bedlam. Nothing seemed real. We lived moment to moment, not knowing what would happen next." She paused.

"And, Father, even though many of the soldiers are Catholic, what they are doing can be described only as diabolical. How can I describe the sacrileges they are committing, right now, even as we speak? Blasphemy. Profanity. Hatred of God.

"Our churches have been closed for almost a year now, and we have been deprived of the sacraments. With all the churches closed and all of us hiding in different locations, we rarely received Communion. We were eight months without the sacraments.

"I have so longed for the Holy Eucharist. This longing consumes me." She stopped, leaned forward, and spoke softly: "They do terrible things to priests, and"—her voice dropped even lower—"and ... to Sisters. It is my hope to bring the younger Sisters here ..." She caught her breath. "To save their ... The soldiers ..." Her voice trailed off.

Father Callahan answered. "I have spoken with many, many refugees already, Mother, so I can tell you that I understand what you have been through. I will help you and the others. You have my commitment to be of any service to you as you relocate here in Los Angeles."

Thank You, my God, for bringing us here and for giving us Father Callahan.

"I'll come by tomorrow about the same time in the afternoon when my work at the chancery office is finished. God bless you, Mother. I'll drop by the chapel for a few moments. I want to pray now."

Chapter 13

An Amazingly Different Lent

*I feel the necessity of prayer. It is my consolation and
hope, because, without the help of God Our Lord, I can
do nothing. I am like a dry stick as regards doing anything
that's good, and bad weeds grow in my soul with great
velocity and strength whenever I neglect prayer.*

—From the spiritual notes of Mother Luisita, 1928

"Did you see Mother Luisita praying in the chapel?"

"Yes. Isn't it remarkable? What does it mean, do you think?
I've never seen anything like it. Do you think anyone else has
noticed?"

The early morning sun filtered through the window, on the
habits of two Immaculate Heart Sisters conversing in the first-
floor hallway.

"Well, I definitely noticed. She kneels for hours at the Communion rail. She almost looks like a statue. After breakfast, I
went into the chapel just for a moment and noticed she was still
there praying. I watched her. She never moved."

Nodding, the other nun added, "Yes, I also noticed. Yesterday,
after supper, she spent hours there, and again this morning as
you just said. She's still there."

IN THE FACE OF DARKNESS

The two Immaculate Heart Sisters looked at each other. "Let's go see her again." They tiptoed up the side aisle and knelt close to the side wall so they could have a better view of their guest. Yes, she was still there. Mother Luisita was kneeling absolutely straight and perfectly still at the Communion rail, eyes fixed on the tabernacle.

The two Sisters stretched as far as they could because they both wanted to see her face again. Yes. There it was: a supernatural light emanating from her face, with a radiance they had never seen before and were at a loss to describe. One thing they did know—it was something angelic, pure, not of this earth.

They drew Sister Teresa aside later in the day and asked her in Spanish, "Does she kneel like this all the time?" Sister Teresa laughed softly. "Who? Oh, you mean our Mother Luisita. Yes, I'm her second cousin, and our whole family has always been aware of her extraordinary devotion to the Blessed Sacrament."

"Sister Teresa, I hope you don't mind if I ask you something personal. Do you see anything, let's say, special, when she kneels there hour after hour?"

Sister Teresa laughed softly again. "Oh, I see. You saw something, didn't you? Well, let me answer with a story. Before we had to close our schools because of the persecution, we would bring the children into Calvary Chapel and teach them how to pray. On the First Friday of each month, we would have a special children's Mass. Well, the children saw what you are seeing and would sneak back into the church when they could during the day, and there she would be, kneeling at the Communion rail with a glowing face. They loved to watch her pray and look at that radiance that the two of you have now witnessed. Especially after receiving Holy Communion, this happens to her. We are all used to it. The people of our town of Atotonilco call her 'our saint.'"

"Wow!"

Sister Teresa continued: "I'll share something with you that our Mother Luisita said to us once. I wrote it down and have meditated on it so many times that I have it memorized. To me, it captures the essence of our Carmelite vocation, our life of prayer and work among God's people. She is our foundress, you know. She said, 'The interior soul knows how to work and remain aware of God's presence in her at the same time. Between Jesus and the soul there flows a current that no one sees and a dialogue that no one hears.' Something resounds within me when I meditate on this thought. I believe there is a connection between these words and this radiance that comes upon her when she prays."

The two Immaculate Heart Sisters left the conversation still wondering.

On Wednesday afternoon, Father Callahan met again with Mother Luisita in the convent parlor.

Father Callahan pulled a notebook from his briefcase, and they sat at a sturdy wooden table.

Father Callahan nodded for Mother Luisita to begin.

Mother Luisita reached for the brown leather bag on the table. "In this bag, Father, I have brought some documents that I'd like to read to you during different parts of my story."

"That would be fine."

She took a deep breath and began.

"I want to backtrack a little, Father. I don't know if you are aware, but I was married for fourteen years to a doctor, Pascual Rojas."

He looked up. "Well, no, Mother, I didn't know that you had been married. I'd like to hear more."

IN THE FACE OF DARKNESS

She continued. "Pascual and I shared many things, but especially a calling to be of service to God's poor. So many people in Mexico live not only in poverty, but in misery. Pascual was also a man of means and came from a well-to-do family. After our marriage, we helped the poor in every way we could, especially the sick. Quietly. Consistently. We both knew we could not selfishly squander our wealth on ourselves. Father, my husband was an excellent doctor, and he was determined to use his skills on the indigent who so desperately needed medical care."

"I see. This is part of the beginning of your community, right, Mother?"

"Yes. I think that knowing this will help you understand as I answer your questions about our ministries, our apostolates.

"One day, some muleteers found an old woman struggling along the road winding through our foothills. She could hardly walk and appeared to be in ill health. Not knowing what else to do, they placed her on the back of one of the mules, and when they reached our little town, they discovered that there was no place to put her and no one to take care of her. So, as a last resort, she was put in the town jail.

"Pascual and I were among the first people to visit her there. Her situation deeply moved many of the people of Atotonilco. Atotonilco el Alto: that's the name of our town."

"Did your town have a hospital, Mother?"

"No, Father. Atotonilco is very small. Nevertheless, the wealthy were well taken care of, but nothing at all was available for the poor. Absolutely nothing. We transferred her to the home of friends, the Romo family, where she received tender, loving care and the Last Rites of the Church during her final days of life."

Mother Luisita looked up. Her face had become more animated as she spoke. "About the same time, our good God was working within the hearts of many people in our parish who had also noticed the plight of the poor. On September 15, 1891, about ten years into our marriage, with the consent of our pastor, together with several other parishioners, Pascual and I held our first meeting to discuss the needs of the poor in our town. Father Celso Sánchez Aldana, our pastor, gave us our name — the Conference of Saint Vincent de Paul under the patronage of the Sacred Heart of Jesus. You could say that our community of Carmelite Sisters was born from this Conference."

Placing one hand on the brown leather bag, she continued: "Our Lord did not bless our marriage with the children we had so longed for. For ten long years, we had made novenas together asking God for a child, but all to no avail. One day Pascual said, 'Luisita, Our Lord has not sent us any children. The poor will be our children.' We both knew that this would be the channel through which we would help the poor. The establishment of our own little hospital came about as a result."

"What year did you say the hospital began?"

"It was 1891. So many people joined in our efforts. Right away, at our first meeting, they elected me as president. Some of the members went together to ask our friend Don Reinaga if he would give us one of his houses to use as a hospital. He was happy to be a part of the project."

Father Callahan leaned forward. "Mother, are you saying that when the people of the parish noticed this need, they just simply got together with their pastor and, with his help and blessing, everyone pitched in and helped?"

"That's exactly what happened. The building needed repairs and additions. Pascual took care of acquiring the funding for this. Little by little, sections were added to the only existing wing. One section was designated as the hospital, and one toward the back was to serve as the living quarters for a future religious community of Sisters we hoped would come and work in our hospital. In time, our beautiful Calvary Chapel occupied a third wing, and the last section became the orphanage and school for the poor."

"Are you saying that, from this parish endeavor, a hospital, a chapel, a school, and an orphanage all came about?" Father Callahan asked. "They were all on the same property?"

"Yes. Here I've noticed you have city blocks. Back in those days, Atotonilco was far more rural, not yet developed. I guess you could say we took up more or less one large city block — one with orchards, that is."

Father Callahan became absorbed in this captivating story of parish teamwork. He sat back in his chair and clasped his hands behind his neck, remaining deep in thought for a few minutes before asking Mother Luisita to continue.

"My husband's brother is a pharmacist, and he offered to fill prescriptions at no charge. Some financial assistance for the hospital was assured on a monthly basis because of the generosity and cooperation of the townspeople. Some of us women learned basic nursing skills. I had already learned much while accompanying Pascual on his rounds."

"Mother Luisita, this is an amazing story you are telling me. Please continue."

"One part of the house was made ready for patients very quickly. About four months later, in January 1892, our Hospital of the Sacred Heart was solemnly blessed. Just about the whole town was present for the blessing. Pascual spoke at the ceremony, and many people wrote down his words. He told everyone, 'The money given to us to bring about this work is like the blood of Christ. It must serve to redeem the world.' The hospital consisted of two reception rooms and two patients' rooms, one for men and one for women, one surgery room, the kitchen, lounge, and an ample patio."

Father Callahan ran his fingers through his hair thoughtfully, musing for a few moments before he said, "Mother, your husband's words move me very much. This is the way all Christians should view their finances. Did people come right away to your hospital?"

Mother Luisita looked up with a smile that lit up her face.

"The sick began arriving. Our first patient was a woman whose illness was the result of her lifestyle. She was sick not only physically, but spiritually. She eventually returned to her home in better health and good spirits.

"This woman became a symbol of our work. We pledged to bring health to both body and spirit. And that is what we continue to do, even now as best we can, despite the takeover of our hospital by the soldiers. I tell you this story, Father, because our community grew out of our little Hospital of the Sacred Heart."

"Before we finish up for today," said Father Callahan, "I want to ask you one last question: What is the connection between the hospital and your community of Sisters?"

"My husband became very sick in 1896, only four years after the establishment of our hospital. We had been married for fourteen years. We traveled to Guadalajara for an operation, but it was not successful. As a doctor, he knew that his case was terminal."

"How long was it, then, from the diagnosis to his death, Mother?"

"Six weeks. The two of us then experienced an amazingly different Lent. I remained in Guadalajara with him. We both knew he didn't have much time left, so we made the most of our last forty days together. You see, Father, he became sick on Ash

Wednesday, and, like Our Lord, he died on Good Friday. We took him back to Atotonilco and buried him on Holy Saturday."

Looking back at Father Callahan, she added simply, "This is Pascual's doctor bag. I had the tremendous privilege of preparing him for death: we had a retreat of seven days together in the hospital, using the Spiritual Exercises of Saint Ignatius. I sat by his chair, and later by his bed, and read to him and prayed with him. We talked about God, about life, about the future, and he was concerned about what I would do after his death.

"All my life I had experienced an inner understanding that I was supposed to do something else during my lifetime. What was this something? I didn't know exactly what it was. As I matured and learned more about the consecrated life, I found it very appealing. In fact, one of my favorite saints is Jane Frances de Chantal, who was married, widowed, and then became a foundress of a religious community. Pascual gave me a biography of her. Saint Jane made a vow of chastity right after her husband died. That's where I got the idea to do the same. Somehow Pascual knew of these inner desires. As he weakened during his last days, he looked up at me and said, 'I know what you will do. You will become a religious.'

"Father Callahan, Pascual told me while he lay there in the hospital, 'I will tell you what things I would like to bequeath to the seminary and then, Luisita, everything I have, I leave for your work.'

"Father Nicholas, a Franciscan priest who was Pascual's cousin, was my support as my husband was dying. He knew about my interior nudging to be a religious, and we had a lot of opportunities to discern together what Our Lord was asking of me."

Father Callahan was beginning to understand that God had sent him a very holy woman. He thoughtfully continued to listen as this chosen soul told her story.

"Father Nicholas agreed to a special request I asked of him during those forty days. He was there with me at Pascual's deathbed.

"Immediately after Pascual's death on Good Friday 1896, Father Nicholas and I went into the adjoining room for a few minutes. He lit a candle and placed it in my hand, as we had agreed. I knelt before the beautiful crucifix that Pascual had given me, and, then and there, I made a vow of chastity in the presence of Father Nicholas.

"On Holy Saturday we took Pascual's body back to our hometown of Atotonilco. Because Atotonilco did not have a train station, we brought his body by train to La Barca, about sixty miles from Guadalajara, and the rest of the way, about thirty miles, to Atotonilco by a horse-drawn coach.

"Our pastor, his altar servers, and nearly three thousand people met us as we approached the town. They had made an improvised altar. Right there in the street, our pastor welcomed the body. I remember that all the townspeople with one voice intoned the responses to the various prayers. Then we all processed to the church where we were married, San Miguel. The funeral Mass was celebrated there with great solemnity. From the church, we all accompanied his body to the municipal cemetery. My grief was very deep.

"After the burial, my mother said, 'Luisita, you are coming home with me.' I took care of Pascual's personal belongings and distributed them to seminarians, as he had requested. I withdrew from many of the normal routines of life and devoted my time to prayer. I wore traditional black clothing because I was already in mourning for my father's death — he died the year before Pascual — so I became somewhat of a hermit and didn't leave my mother's house.

"My mother told me, 'Luisita, your grieving is too extreme.'"

IN THE FACE OF DARKNESS

Father Callahan looked at his watch. "Time passes quickly when I am with you, Mother Luisita. I need a little time now to process what you have just told me, and I would like to pray. So, let's conclude for today with a visit to the Blessed Sacrament. I'll be back tomorrow to hear more of your story."

Sunlight no longer filled the convent parlor. Dusk was approaching as the two walked down the hallway together and turned into the doorway of the convent chapel to pray.

Chapter 14

The Widow with a Basket

*The interior soul knows how to work and live
and remain recollected at the same time.*

—From the spiritual notes of Mother Luisita

Sister Gertrude held up a children's picture book as the three Carmelites sat in a semicircle in front of her, repeating the English words as she pointed to each picture. They heard a knock. One of the Sisters peeked into the room and said, "Excuse me. Father Callahan is here to see Mother Luisita."

"Thank you, Sister. Well, Mother, we'll continue tomorrow if that is all right with you."

Mother Luisita had not understood one word. Sister Margarita María translated what Sister Gertrude had said.

"Yes, tomorrow," replied Mother Luisita.

How frustrating it is not to understand the simplest words!

One of the Sisters brought a pitcher of ice water to the parlor. Mother Luisita took a sip of water, followed by a deep breath, and continued her conversation from the previous day.

"Following my husband's death—the same year he died, 1896—I applied to enter the Visitation Convent in Morelia, but they didn't accept me because of my poor health.

IN THE FACE OF DARKNESS

"Soon after that, my mother told me that enough was enough. I had mourned Pascual long enough, and she was going to take me on a vacation. So we traveled for several weeks. After the long vacation, I left the darkened room where I had been spending my time and returned to society. I began to check on the hospital daily."

Father Callahan nodded and waited quietly for her to continue.

"In the area of Jalisco, where I was born and raised, there are many hills. The narrow, winding paths up and down these hills cannot be navigated on horseback. We use donkeys. As a widow, I began to leave the house every day and travel either on foot or by donkey through these winding paths to the higher altitudes. I would often bring one of the servants with me. The townspeople named me 'the doctor's widow with the basket always hanging from her arm.'"

Father Callahan shook his head incredulously at the thought of this beautifully cultured woman weaving through the dusty hills on a donkey.

"There were and still are so many very poor people living in caves and makeshift dwellings throughout Los Altos. I brought them food and medicine. We would pray together. I even had some rope to make a swing for the children. Can you imagine little children who didn't know how to play?"

He just shook his head. "Mother Luisita, you've been a married woman, a widow, a foundress, and now a refugee. You have lived a very full life, haven't you, in your corner of the Lord's vineyard?"

"I guess I have, Father. I'm so used to just living it day by day. After my husband's death, I went to our pastor and told him that I wanted to build a memorial for Pascual. He convinced me that I should construct a chapel in his memory. So, with Pascual's inheritance, with his stocks and the value of the books in his extensive library, I had our beautiful Calvary Chapel built right next to the hospital.

"I placed the first stone myself in 1900. We were able to get the noted Italian architect Adamo Boari to design the chapel."

"Isn't he the architect of Mexico City's famous Palacio de Bellas Artes, still under construction?" Father Callahan asked.

"That's right. He is very gifted. Our chapel was finished in 1903, and the construction for the Palacio began in 1904.

"Father, we had a large orchard behind the chapel. The orchard got smaller and smaller as we expanded our services. As I mentioned yesterday, I had envisioned one part of the property as a residence for a community of Sisters who would work at the hospital at some future time. Another wing was built to be an elementary school for poor children. My younger sister Concepción donated the funds to enlarge the original hospital building.

"With the chapel finished in 1903, I began to look actively again into the possibility of entering a convent. Our Lord led me to the cloistered Carmelite nuns at the Monastery of Saint Teresa in Guadalajara, the same community with three nuns living in Hollywood as refugees like us. I know these Sisters.

"On March 3, 1904, when I was almost thirty-eight, I entered the Carmelite monastery in Guadalajara. As I look back on it now, I see that Our Lord cleared the way for me to absorb Carmelite spirituality in that holy place. The nuns were very observant of the Rule, and their prioress was known for her holiness. The monastery had come from one of Saint Teresa's monasteries in Spain, and the nuns there accepted me despite my age and poor health.

"Three weeks later, on March 28, 1904, according to the custom at that time, I became a novice and was given the holy habit of Carmel and my new name of Sister María Dolores of the Blessed Sacrament."

"How long was it from your entrance to your new name and receiving the habit, Mother?"

"Three weeks. I loved everything about Carmel. Mother Refugio was the prioress. As I just mentioned, Father, because of my age and my poor health, God permitted that I was granted certain mitigations from the Rule and adaptations so that I could enter there."

"How long did you remain in the Guadalajara monastery, Mother?"

"Three months. I had long talks with Mother Refugio. She saw right away that I had a Carmelite vocation, and at the same time we both discerned a strong interior calling within me to help the sick and the children. We understood each other.

"One day I had an experience, a kind of dream, in which I seemed to see children calling to me and saying, 'Your soul is saved. But what about our souls?' To this day I still can't get these words out of my mind."

Father Callahan shifted in his chair. "Did any other dreams come to you while you were in Carmel, Mother?"

"Another time, while I was at prayer, an image of small children playing in a park came into my mind, and a group of Sisters was looking after them. I felt they were calling out to me to come to them.

"Again in a dream, I saw myself wearing the Carmelite habit among children and the sick, who talked with me as I was walking. At other times, I saw myself wearing a habit with a white mantle. I didn't understand. These types of intuitions or images, whatever you want to call them, continued. But what did it all mean?"

Father Callahan looked at her intently and asked, "Did anyone help you discern these intuitions?"

"Yes, Father. During the three months I was in the monastery, I had several conversations with my archbishop, José de Jesús Ortíz. I told him that, on the one hand, I was happy and felt completely at home in the monastery. On the other hand, my thoughts would turn to Atotonilco and the welfare of the people who needed help so desperately. I also spoke many times with my pastor, Father Celso Sánchez Aldana. I found out that a lot of things had been going poorly at the hospital since I left.

"I left the monastery in June 1904, with the approval of Archbishop Ortíz, who also discerned that I should leave the cloister. Father Aldana had encouraged me to return and to finish the work I had begun there. He told me I should continue as I had before, with the hope that more women would join me and in time we would be the founders of a new religious community in Atotonilco dedicated to serving the poor and the sick."

"What year was that again?"

"It was 1904."

"I would like to know what kind of work your Sisters have been doing since 1904, when you returned. I understand you are not cloistered nuns, who remain secluded within their monasteries, yet you are Carmelites. Tell me more about the ministries of the community you have founded."

"Father Callahan, our main ministry, or apostolate, is prayer. Our active works are health care and education, especially for the poor and for children."

Father Callahan nodded. "How did you begin these apostolates?"

"Health care began in 1892. Education began in 1904. We staffed a private school in Atotonilco that our previous pastor,

Father José Refugio Huerta, began. We staffed it for some time, and it officially became an apostolate of the community in 1919. We had also opened the Little School of the Spelling Book in 1918. Before the persecution became violent, we opened schools in Atotonilco, San Francisco de Asís, and Ocotlán. We had been preparing to open a school in Guadalajara when the persecution broke out. We opened the orphanage formally in 1919, but we had already been caring for orphans for many years."

"Mother, when did you become Carmelites?"

"Not until 1921, after we asked Archbishop Orozco y Jiménez if he would allow us to become what was known as Carmelite Tertiaries, the Carmelite Third Order Religious. I have a copy of the letter I sent to the archbishop here in this bag. I keep all of my correspondence and important papers in it.

"On July 31, 1926, last year, the federal soldiers took over the hospital. A few of our Sisters stayed there to continue their work as nurses and to look out for our interests. We also had to close the schools at Atotonilco, San Francisco de Asís, and Octolán. Since then, we've been teaching quietly in private homes and sometimes outdoors in the nearby countryside."

"I see," said Father Callahan. "And what is your goal in coming to the United States?"

"The immediate goal is to have a safe place, a refuge, where the Sisters can come. The persecution has left its mark on many of them. Some have become quite nervous and very anxious. Others are now sick. Above all, I want to bring as many of the younger Sisters here as soon as possible. I am deathly afraid of what might happen to them if they stay. At this time, my long-range goal is to return to Mexico when the persecution quiets down.

"I myself need to hide here in California, as my name is on the government's list of Mexican families who are landowners.

The Widow with a Basket

My family owns much land and is quite wealthy, and because I, too, am a de la Peña, I am being hunted down, Father, and I am very much afraid. I have spoken to our archbishop, and I am following his advice in this matter."

As Mother Luisita spoke of the shadows of persecution stretching across her country and its people, the late-afternoon shadows stretched across the parlor floor.

Father Callahan put his notebook back into his briefcase. Mother Luisita lifted her brown leather bag. As they turned and began walking to the parlor door, Father looked at Mother Luisita and said, "Tomorrow, Mother. I'll be back tomorrow."

They entered the chapel and knelt down together.

Chapter 15

The Curved Path

It would help you very much if you would read The
Way of Perfection *by our Holy Mother Saint Teresa
and* The Precautions *of Saint John of the Cross
rather than books of mere sentimentality.*

—Letter to Sister Margarita María, 1932

It was the second of July, and Mother Luisita was sitting in her
second-floor room, alone with her thoughts, listening to the
soothing patter of the raindrops on the leaves of the tree outside.
Her eyes were closed lightly; her hands clasped quietly. She was
praying. One of the Sisters kept coming into her mind.

I wonder how Sister Refugio is doing. I'm worried.

She picked up her pen and began writing slowly, deliberately
using the code she had developed since the beginning of the
Cristiada, first to Sister Refugio and then to the other Sisters
who had written her.

Her advice was down-to-earth, practical, and dotted with
spiritual wisdom. To one person she wrote, "Do not fear, in spite
of the scarecrows that the devil is placing on your path." To
another, "Pray that Our Lord will help us, and that He will be
pleased with us. That's the only thing that should really matter

to us, and as far as everything else is concerned, none of it counts for anything. All these other things are like flowers that bloom only for a day."

Sister Teresa knocked on her door. Mother spoke first. "Sister Teresa, I'm worried about Sister Refugio. I am writing to her. I've decided that she will be in the next group of five Sisters who will come up to Los Angeles."

Sister Teresa was relieved to hear this. "I'm worried too, Mother. I'd like to meet her at the station if that's all right with you."

Mother Luisita nodded.

"Sister Gertrude would like to see us in ten minutes in her office, Mother. That's why I knocked on the door."

Sister Gertrude called the three Carmelites into her office as soon as they knocked. "Sisters, we are planning something special for you: a picnic with your cloistered Carmelite nuns from the Monastery of Saint Teresa in Guadalajara. The Sisters at our Hollywood convent are planning everything. I'll let you know more details soon. That's all I know about it so far."

The doorbell rang. Mother Luisita stood up and then turned toward the group of Sisters.

"Father Callahan," said Mother Luisita, and she excused herself and left the room.

Father Callahan was waiting for Mother Luisita in the parlor.

"Good afternoon, Mother. How are you?" He smiled.

"Very well, thanks be to God." Mother Luisita returned the smile.

"Mother, I'm hoping that today we can finish up with our get-acquainted chats, and tomorrow I would like to speak with you and Sisters Teresa and Margarita María. After that, I will go ahead and begin right away looking for suitable lodging and work for your Sisters.

"Today I'd like to learn more about your community—your typical daily schedule and in what ways your community is similar to and different from the cloistered Carmelites."

Nodding, Mother Luisita pulled her brown bag a little closer. "Yes. I will tell you about that. As I mentioned the other day, I left the cloister in June 1904 and returned to my hometown of Atotonilco el Alto. I spoke often with our pastor. Several women came to help me, and together we began to put some order back into the hospital. You see," she looked up at Father Callahan, "during the three months I was in the monastery in Guadalajara, the hospital had fallen into a state of general disrepair.

"When our pastor traveled to Guadalajara to make his yearly retreat, he spoke to the archbishop about us. After he returned, he told us that Archbishop Ortiz was favorable to having our group begin the process of becoming a canonical community in the Church.[11]

"On December 24, 1904, the beginning of our new community was confirmed, and on Christmas evening at six o'clock, five women and I dedicated ourselves without public vows to the care of the sick and the education of children. Father Medrano, our pastor, told us, 'If this work is pleasing to God, the number of members will increase. If not, it will be dissolved.'

---

[11] In this case, *canonical* refers to the Catholic Church's acceptance of the new association of Mother Luisita and the founding Sisters and the authorization of the association to work within the Church. A community's founder, such as Mother Luisita, receives from the Holy Spirit the gift of a charism, a group of graces that embody the spirit and mission of a religious community. The members live the charism. Church authority discerns the authenticity of the association and gives it juridical status.

"He then said that I was to be called Mother Luisita and the other ladies now had the title 'Sister,' and we were to pattern our way of life on the life of the cloistered monasteries as closely as possible. Our pastor demanded that church rules regarding what areas of the house would be private and rules regarding our leaving the house known as strict enclosure be observed.[12]

"A new pastor, Father Arnulfo Jiménez, arrived in 1905. He made many changes and lifted the rule of strict enclosure. Father Callahan, we had been living the life of cloistered nuns and also worked a full schedule. Although our beautiful Carmelite way of life appealed to us, our daily schedule was not yet balanced. I became sick and went to Guadalajara for a few months to recuperate. While I was there, I took advantage of the opportunity to discuss matters related to our new community with Archbishop Ortíz, who was very interested in learning more about us."

"Mother, did all of these changes have a bearing on your health then?"

"Yes, they did. While I was recuperating in Guadalajara, I also spoke with the archbishop regarding church law and my inheritance. Part of my possessions were to be used for the foundation in Atotonilco. He also offered to give us a rule of life to follow that would suit the purpose for which our community

[12] Enclosed religious orders of Catholic nuns have solemn vows with a strict separation from the affairs of the external world. The term *cloistered* is synonymous with *enclosed*. In the Catholic Church, enclosure is regulated by the *Code of Canon Law*, either the Latin code or the Oriental code, and also by subsidiary legislation. Congregation for Institutes of Consecrated Life and for Societies of Apostolic Life, *Verbi Sponsa: Instruction on the Contemplative Life and on the Enclosure of Nuns* (May 13, 1999), http://www. vatican.va/roman_curia/congregations/ccscrlife/documents/ rc_con_ccscrlife_doc_13051999_verbi-sponsa_en.html

was founded. Remember, Father, when you asked me about our apostolic works?"

He nodded.

"I will answer now in the words of Archbishop Ortíz as he expressed it in our original Rule given to us and signed by him in 1909."

Mother Luisita paused and closed her eyes. Then, in her cultured, quiet voice, she said with much reverence, "We were founded primarily 'to make reparation to the Blessed Sacrament, to spread the love of God, to attend to the needs of the sick and the instruction of children.' We followed quite a curved path after that, Father Callahan. I say curved because, over and over again, the path we were following kept changing through the requests of the archbishop."

Father Callahan raised his eyebrows.

"Archbishop Ortíz told us, soon after we received our Rule, that we would have to join the Sisters of Perpetual Adoration. I was very surprised, but we obeyed. We received a sample of the habits of that community. The Sisters dressed a doll in the habit of their community and sent it to me. This was the method used in those days.

"The archbishop had already received the official prescript from Rome authorizing our joining the Sisters of Perpetual Adoration when he died suddenly and everything stopped. The year was 1912, and our status remained at a standstill."

"So, what happened next, Mother?"

"Our new archbishop, Francisco Orozco y Jiménez, arrived, and he asked us to join yet a different community, the Sisters Servants of the Most Blessed Sacrament. Archbishop Orozco y Jiménez told us that the Vatican had asked the bishops to consolidate small communities. Rome had said that merging smaller communities was better than having so many isolated groups springing up throughout the Church. That, too, influenced his decision for us to annex ourselves to an existing community.

"By then, it was May of 1913, and the Mexican Revolution, which had begun in 1910, had become more violent, more dangerous. The archbishop didn't want us to end up struggling in an outlying rural area amid the violence. Our lives were truly in danger, and his thinking was that we would be safer if we merged with another community.[13] I met with both our new archbishop and the superior of the Sisters Servants of the Most Blessed Sacrament to finalize the plans for our community to become a part of theirs. Father Silviano Carrillo, their founder, was also present at the meeting. Legal proceedings regarding the annexation, such as the transferring of money and property, followed after that, and then Father Carrillo called us to a retreat that would begin on the Solemnity of Corpus Christi."

"Did they have many convents?"

"Well, Father Callahan, because of the very real danger to all Catholic priests and Sisters during the Revolution, we had to hide in order to save our lives. So, to answer your question, yes, we moved to their house in Zapotlán, but beginning in August 1914, we were told to disperse and live in private homes with

[13] Elena Poniatowska gives an example of the atrocities committed during the Mexican Revolution (1910–1920): "The Carrancistas [soldiers of Venustiano Carranza] captured fifty nuns. 'After a certain amount of time passed, they dropped them off at a hospital "where they bore their offspring."'" Elena Poniatowska, *Las Soldaderas*, trans. David Dorado Romo (El Paso: Cinco Punto Press, 2006), quoted in Jim Cook, "*Las Soldaderas*: Women of the Mexican Revolution," *Jim and Carole's Mexico Adventure* (blog), November 15, 2012, http://cookjmex.blogspot.com/2012/11/las-soldaderas-women-of-Mexican.html.

trusted families. I made my profession of vows in a private home and was given the name Sister Juana Francisca of the Blessed Sacrament because of my devotion to Saint Jane Frances de Chantal. Those were very perilous times, Father."

She leaned over, picked up the weathered doctor's bag, and placed it on the table. "When I am tempted to any kind of discouragement, I like to pull out a letter from the pastor who witnessed our first promises in 1904. He wrote it at the time of our annexation. It gives me peace and the courage to continue. May I share it with you?"

"Of course, Mother." Father Callahan took the faded paper and read it slowly. From time to time he nodded assent, and at other times he shook his head with compassion.

Do not fear. For a long time, you have been serving the Lord and have asked Him to let you know His will. It has been made manifest to you very clearly, and now, "Down to work." He will lead you with much care and great love, because He cannot fail in His promises.

So, blindly and with utter confidence, you should place yourselves in the hands of God. Neither the house, nor the habit, this or that Order, should attract you. Only what God wants.

What I told all the founders together in that little garden, I repeat now and shall always repeat it: "May this Community, which is God's garden, be formed with the end to please God and to become holy."

He will know how and in what manner He would water His little garden, and if it is His pleasure to destroy it (something which I do not fear), it will also be good, since we belong to God.

Your old and useless chaplain, who blesses you and wishes abundance of graces in the Community, new in form, but old in spirit,

Rev. Arcadio Medrano[14]

After a moment of silence, Mother Luisita continued. "We were twenty Sisters at that time, and all twenty remained with the Sisters Servants until the Solemnity of Corpus Christi in 1917. During this fourth year, a number of factors converged that led me to consider leaving the Sisters Servants.

"I collaborated with Archbishop Orozco y Jiménez and my pastor in Atotonilco and the superiors of the Sisters Servants. The archbishop suggested that I begin an eight-day Ignatian retreat to discern what I should do. He sent a priest to give me the Spiritual Exercises of Saint Ignatius. I prayed and deliberated, and at the conclusion of the eight days, I asked permission to leave the community and return to Atotonilco. Archbishop Orozco y Jiménez gave me permission. I have the letter here with me."

Mother Luisita searched through her bag, brought out the letter, and handed it to Father Callahan. He read the first part of it aloud.

Reverend Mother Juana Francisca: Guadalajara, Jalisco

May 22, 1917

In view of the reasons explained, I wish to let you know, that you, as well as the Religious who with you were incorporated to the Servants of Jesus, are granted the

---

[14] From *Positio Super Virtutibus: Canonizationis Servae Dei Maríae Aloisiae Iosephace a SS. Sacramento*, English ed. (Rome: Tipografia Guerra, 1991), 19–20.

necessary permission to separate from the above Institute and return to Atotonilco el Alto. May God keep your Reverence for many years.

Manuel Alvarado, Vicar General[15]

"Father, out of the twenty Sisters who had joined the Sisters Servants with me in 1914, only three returned to Atotonilco with me. The rest remained in the other community. A few more women joined us when they learned we had returned. And we began again."

"Yes, Mother. And this curved path has now brought you to Los Angeles as a refugee."

Mother Luisita sighed softly. "Yes."

He looked off into the distance, thinking. "Mother, tonight I am going to look over my notes from our conversations and pray for guidance regarding what to do. Shall we end today's visit in the chapel?"

"Yes, and I will be praying especially for you."

"To begin again seems to be the theme of your whole life, Mother."

"Or perhaps, Father, the theme could also be *Fiat*, 'be it done unto me according to Your word.'"

And they left the parlor together.

---

[15] Ibid., 22.

Chapter 16

Free to Serve

*Try not to worry. Everything in life has its ups and downs, yet
above everything else, we must live a life of faith, seeing all
things as coming from the hand of God and for our own good.*

—Letter to Mother Mary, 1933

"Sisters, we're off to Hollywood!"

Early in the morning of July 16, picnic baskets in hand, the
Sisters got into the car, eager for a special day with their friends,
the exiled cloistered Carmelites from the Monastery of Saint
Teresa in Guadalajara, the community that Mother Luisita had
joined about twenty years earlier. The day would begin with a
special Mass with the cloistered nuns, celebrated by a Mexican
priest at the Immaculate Heart motherhouse in Hollywood.

The car maneuvered through the Hollywood hills at a speedy
clip to get there on time for the special Mass. At the chapel, the
Sisters got out of the car and put on their white mantles. Just
ahead of them, near the chapel entrance, three cloistered refugees—Mother Teresa of Jesus, Mother Magdalena of the Sacred
Heart, and Sister Rosa María of Carmel—waited to greet them.

No words were exchanged. Mother Luisita's eyes looked deeply
into the eyes of each nun, wrapping each in her silent empathy

and support. They understood. Each knew what the other had been through. That understanding found expression in the long, quiet embrace in which persecuted persons recognize and affirm the suffering undergone by others.

Then they entered the chapel.

Mother Luisita genuflected and knelt down, and fixing her eyes on the tabernacle, she prayed. To be free to enter a chapel, to attend Mass with the sermon in her beautiful Spanish language, and to receive Holy Communion with the nuns of the Saint Teresa Carmel in Guadalajara was a gift beyond measure. It seemed to her that Mass was over in the blink of an eye.

Is Mass over already? It seemed too short today. Where did the time go?

Afterward, the two communities were driven in two cars to a secluded little park in Hollywood, where they spent the day together. The Sisters in the Hollywood convent had also brought a picnic basket. Although there was an abundance of food, the Sisters were hungrier for news of the other Sisters, and of their beloved Mexico.

It feels good to speak Spanish again!

In the 1500s, Saint Teresa of Jesus established seventeen monasteries. One of these was the monastery of San José de Caravaca de la Cruz, in the province of Murcia, Spain. The Caravaca monastery established a Carmel in Puebla, Mexico, in 1604. In 1695, six Carmelite nuns set out from the Puebla monastery to establish the Carmel of Saint Teresa in Guadalajara, Jalisco, Mexico. Mother Luisita had entered and subsequently left the Guadalajara Carmel in 1904.

I know these nuns.

I love these nuns.

There was so much she wanted to share.

Still, if the truth be told, there were more tears than words. Both communities cried together as they tried to reconstruct the amazing events that had propelled them to California, changing their lives.

"When did you leave Mexico?" Mother Luisita asked.

"We left on the feast of Saint Simon Stock, May 16. When did you leave?" Mother Teresa of Jesus asked.

"We left about five weeks after you, on June 20," Mother Luisita replied.

Sister Rosa Maria asked them, "Did you see the dead bodies hanging from the poles?"

"Yes," came the barely audible reply. They turned their heads away from her.

"Is Father Callahan helping you?" asked Sister Margarita María, breaking the silence.

"He helped us at first, but Father Dennis Kavanaugh, a Jesuit from San Francisco, is helping us now. In fact, as we speak, he is arranging for us to go to San Francisco to live. Archbishop Edward Hanna of San Francisco and Father Edward Whelan, Father Kavanaugh's superior, the rector of Saint Ignatius College, are working out the arrangements. The three of us will go first, and the nuns in Guadalajara will come later.

"The Jesuits in San Francisco will be conducting a triduum before the feast of the Little Flower, and they will use the funds from the donations given to them to bring up all the nuns still in Guadalajara to San Francisco."

Like all refugees, they would go wherever sanctuary was offered them. The circumstances of life would soon split them up again into different cities.

The six women enjoyed their day together, catching up on friends and family, strolling through the secluded park, feeding crumbs to the little birds and small foxes that ventured close enough to be fed, and basking in the light and strength of friendships that had endured despite the difficult times. Theirs was the tight bond that forms among those who have suffered together.

"Even the little animals are treated with respect in this country," offered Sister Teresa, observing the interaction between God's creatures and the people strolling and playing in the park.

As the shadows from the park's pines and palms began to lengthen, the six refugees reluctantly packed up and headed back to the car. They dropped off the cloistered nuns at the motherhouse and continued on until they reached their convent on Green Avenue.

The following day, Father Callahan spoke with the three refugees. "Beginning today, I will work on your behalf with the pastors in the Los Angeles Diocese to see what kind of ministry we can find for you. The obstacle, of course, is that you don't speak English, but God has brought you this far, Sisters, and I'm sure He'll bring you to the right place here in Los Angeles."

He paused and searched their faces. Yes, their faces had filled out some, and no longer had that gaunt, tight look of malnutrition. Still, he was able to see more — the integrity, stamina, and suffering etched in the faces of these women.

"The other reason I asked to speak with you today," said Father Callahan, "is that I would also like to touch briefly on a sensitive issue — prejudice. I know that you are aware that prejudice and discrimination are found throughout our world. Dear Sisters, prejudice exists in Los Angeles, and you will probably experience it firsthand. You will find it scattered throughout secular society, and I want you to be aware that you may even encounter it in some Catholic churches. In some churches, even Catholic parishes, I've heard it said that Mexican immigrants are told to sit only in the back pews of the church. I hope you will never encounter this discrimination, which I abhor, but I feel it my duty to mention it beforehand, in case you do. Your thoughts on this, Sisters?"

The three exiles smiled wryly.

Prejudice? They knew about prejudice firsthand.

Mother Luisita looked at the two Sisters and then back at Father Callahan.

"Father, in 1917, in the waning of the Mexican Revolution, our newly revised Mexican constitution was adopted by the government. It contained the articles that discriminated against Catholics in Mexico.[16] These horrendous articles took away our religious freedom. At first, they were not implemented so much. Afterward, President Calles enforced them ruthlessly. That's why we are here in the United States, Father. We are more than aware that prejudice, in one form or another, exists all over the world, and that would include Los Angeles. We know that. May God reward you for reminding us of this fact. But know, dear Father Callahan, that nothing in this beautiful country can come close to the hate-filled, diabolical intolerance and discrimination we have experienced! Absolutely nothing!

"And, Father, that is precisely why we are here in this room with you now. That is why we came to your wonderful country as refugees asking for assistance, seeking only religious freedom for ourselves and the freedom to serve."

---

[16] See appendix E for these articles of the Mexican constitution that discriminated against Catholics in Mexico.

IN THE FACE OF DARKNESS

One year had passed since July 31, 1926, the day the bishops of Mexico had closed all the Catholic churches in Mexico and had watched the government destroy everything they had accomplished.

About five weeks after his conversation with the three Sisters—approximately one year after the anticlerical laws were issued—Father Callahan finally had good news to tell the Carmelite refugees:

"Sisters, you have a home."

Although they had waited eagerly for this news for three months, it still came as a surprise. Father Callahan smiled. "Believe it. Believe it. It's true. Sisters, I am so very happy for you."

In his humility, he did not mention how difficult it had been to find lodging and work for them.

"Can you tell us more, Father?" asked Mother Luisita.

"Sisters, you are all going to Holy Innocents Parish in Long Beach, a coastal city about twenty-five miles south of here, to a parish with many Mexican immigrants and a wonderful pastor. His name is Father Francis Ott. The parish is new, established only four years ago in 1923. Father Ott is a very dynamic pastor.

"It will take a few days for the two of us to arrange the details. Plan to leave Los Angeles on Wednesday, August 3. I'll come for you about ten in the morning. As soon as I find out more details, I'll let you know."

Father Callahan and Father Ott were both young priests; Father Ott, only seven years ordained, was just thirty-three, and Father Callahan, three years ordained, was only twenty-nine. Father Callahan had studied at the North American College in Rome and received his doctorate from Fribourg University in Switzerland. His dissertation was on the early life of Father Junípero Serra, who established the California missions. He was especially sensitive to the situation of the Mexican refugees and to the Church's obligation to care for them. It gave him much joy and a great deal of personal satisfaction to help the Carmelites.

It didn't take long to say good-bye to the gracious Immaculate Heart Sisters. Nor did it take very long for the Carmelites to gather their few items together. Their three bedrooms had been cleaned thoroughly. Sister Teresa and Sister Margarita María had worked together to clean Mother Luisita's room, leaving it spotless. Their kind hostesses had given them containers filled to the brim with additional clothing and personal items.

Father Callahan knocked on the convent door at ten in the morning. As soon as the luggage was in the car, he motioned for Mother Luisita to take the front seat. He had decided to drive them to Long Beach himself.

After praying for a safe trip, Father Callahan began to point out places of interest. "Sisters, did you know that the Mexican population of Los Angeles will soon be greater than that of Guadalajara? So don't feel isolated or alone, because you are not. Just wait, and you will see how many refugees are in Long Beach."

The Sisters had no idea so many Mexicans had fled to Los Angeles.

"Sisters, are you aware of the special relationship that exists between the Archdiocese of Guadalajara and the Diocese of Los Angeles?" asked Father Callahan. "If you aren't, I'll be glad to tell you about it."

Mother Luisita answered, "We would like to hear."

"Father Junípero Serra was a Franciscan priest from Spain who brought the Catholic Faith to California. He established the famous California missions from 1769 to 1784. At that time, California still belonged to Mexico, and Father Serra reported to his Franciscan superiors there. The Southwest, including Los

Angeles, belonged specifically to the Archdiocese of Guadalajara. Whenever Father Serra needed anything—material or spiritual—it was fifteen hundred miles away, in Guadalajara."

Mother Luisita looked back at the two Sisters as if to say that they were very aware of the length of that journey, which was similar to the one they had just made.

Father Callahan continued. "During Holy Week each year, the Archbishop of Guadalajara would bless the holy chrism oils[17] and hand them over to one of the Franciscans, who would carry them all the way to California, despite the great distance—which was quite a trek in those days—on horseback, mule, and by foot in some places. This continued for over a hundred years until California was ceded to the United States in 1848. Since then, there has been mutual support between the two cities. Bishop Cantwell is a very good friend of Archbishop Orozco y Jiménez."

I can't even imagine making that journey by walking. What stamina and determination!

"And, Sisters, I know something that most people don't know. About 150 years before the Franciscans came to California, another order arrived first: the Carmelites! On November

---

[17] "On Holy Thursday morning, the bishops, joined by the priests of the diocese, gather at the cathedral to celebrate the Chrism Mass. This Mass manifests the unity of the priests with their bishop. Here the bishop blesses three oils—the Oil of Catechumens (*Oleum Catechumenorum* or *Oleum Sanctorum*), the Oil of the Infirm (Oleum Infirmorum) and Holy Chrism (*Sacrum Chrisma*)—which will be used in the administration of the sacraments throughout the diocese for the year." Father William Saunders, "The Use of Sacramental Oils," *Arlington Catholic Herald*, reprinted at Catholic Education Resource Center, https://www.catholiceducation.org/en/culture/catholic-contributions/the-use-of-sacramental-oils.html.

12, 1602, in what is now San Diego, Father Antonio de la Ascensión celebrated the first Mass in California, attended by the ship's crew, two other Carmelite priests, and about one hundred local Native Americans. Yes, all the cities up and down the coast that were named after saints — San Diego, Santa Cruz, Santa Barbara — were named by or connected in some way to the Carmelites."[18]

∞

The group continued their drive in silence until Father Callahan announced, "We're nearing Long Beach now. Would you like to hear more about the parish?"

"Yes, please, Father."

"Here's some more history. Holy Innocents is a very new parish. It was formally established by Bishop Cantwell on December 12, 1923, the feast of Our Lady of Guadalupe. The parish's name was supposed to be Saint Luke's, but the Episcopalians built a church in Long Beach at the same time and called it Saint Luke's, so the name of our new church was changed quickly to Holy Innocents."

He turned the corner.

"Look, Sisters, here we are. It's just a minute or two down this street."

---

[18] Author's interview with Father Philip Sullivan, O.C.D., in 2015 after he presented the Carmelite Sisters of the Most Sacred Heart of Los Angeles with the icon that he wrote of the first Mass in California, celebrated by Father Antonio de la Ascensión, O.C.D.

Chapter 17

When the Waves Come

For Your glory, I am happy to put myself and all my loved
ones and everything I possess totally at Your service.

—From the spiritual notes of Mother Luisita

After driving one more block, Father Callahan stopped his car. "Here we are, Sisters. Do you see the white church on your left? That's Holy Innocents. I'll take you inside. Just leave your luggage in the car. We'll take care of it when we reach our final destination."

As they got out of the car, the briny sea breeze brushed against their faces. Even on this hot August day, they could feel the ocean moisture in the air. Looking around, they entered the interior of the church, which was quite simple with its wooden pews, softly muted colors, and a lovely natural wood backdrop behind the altar. Holy Innocents Church still retained a tinge of that delicious fragrance of newly cut wood. Light filled the nave, and simple, devotional statues of Our Lady and Saint Joseph graced the alcoves on the left and right sides of the sanctuary.

But what drew them straight ahead was the sanctuary with its traditional, architectural central point—the tabernacle with its Eucharistic Presence—to which everything else was directed.

"Stay here a few moments, Sisters, while I wait for Father Ott outside."

As soon as she knelt down, Mother Luisita felt at home in this little, white stucco church bathed in such peace. As she closed her eyes and prayed, she began to notice birds singing in the nearby trees.

Birds! It has been so long since I've heard them chirping. I have missed them so much. When the fighting began, they all flew away. They scattered. How I wish I could bottle up their singing and send it right now to my Sisters in Mexico.

The silence in the church was profound. It was nearing midday, and they were the only ones there. The soft light, the singing birds, and, above all else, the presence of Our Lord in the Blessed Sacrament brought a calmness to the refugees.

Mother Luisita continued to pray.

We flew away, too, didn't we, Lord? We scattered.

Here in the United States, Lord, will we sing again?

She heard Father Callahan's footsteps coming closer and turned around. "Mother, Father Francis Ott is in the back of the church waiting for you. Let me introduce him to you."

He led the way. Father Ott knew only a little Spanish, and Father Callahan helped him through a bilingual introduction. "Please tell the Sisters that I look forward to their coming to our parish. I'm trying to learn some more Spanish so I can converse with them more easily." He gave Mother Luisita a warm smile that could be understood in any language.

Father Callahan translated.

Mother Luisita smiled graciously. "Please convey to Father Ott our heartfelt gratitude for accepting us into his parish, and let him know we are hard workers and want to bring our skills and talents into this new land."

Turning to Father Ott, she added, "We are at your service, Father."

Father Callahan translated.

Smiling, Father Ott replied, "Sisters, I know my Spanish is nowhere near good enough to communicate with you effectively. A few basic words, some basic phrases, that's all. But with Sister Margarita's help, I'll try my best! We are going now to meet the Flores family. You'll be staying with them."

Father Callahan repeated his words in Spanish and then added, "Father Ott has been praying for Spanish-speaking catechists to come to the parish. And here you are! He wants you to take a parish census and find out how many Mexican immigrants are Catholic and what they need, and then to evangelize and catechize them as necessary."

The Sisters smiled broadly. The way things were working out through God's divine providence was utterly amazing.

Missionaries. This is who we are! We can do this. Yes, we can do this!

Father Callahan continued, "Sisters, the house where you will be staying has been named 'the Christian Soldiers' Home' by the neighbors. Many bishops, priests, nuns, and laypeople — all refugees like you — have stayed with Doña Nicolasa and her three adult children who live with her."

Doña Nicolasa was waiting for them on the front porch. She walked toward the Sisters and embraced them warmly. "Sisters, I'm from Guadalajara, too, and one of my sons was born in Atotonilco. And look who is waiting for you in our living room!"

Doña Nicolasa opened the front door and motioned for Mother to enter first. The other Sisters followed.

"Oh, my daughters! Look!" Mother Luisita exclaimed as she stepped inside. The three exiles gazed open-mouthed in astonishment. Right there in the living room on the central wall was a painting of the Virgin of the Incarnation. It was an exact replica of the original, which is found in the little chapel of the Holy Family, a few miles from Atotonilco el Alto and accessible only on horseback.

"Doña Nicolasa, you know about the little chapel of the Holy Family near Atotonilco?" Mother asked incredulously.

"Know about it! My two sons—you'll meet them tonight —used to serve Mass in that little chapel. I got the idea this morning to hang the painting right there—front and center—so it would be the first thing you would see when you arrived. It was a real inspiration, don't you think?" Hands on her hips, she stood there quite pleased with herself as she took in the same scene playing out in her home once again—this time with these dear Carmelite refugees.

Mother Luisita didn't answer because she was crying. Over the next few hours, in the charming backyard of the Flores home, with its fruit trees and hanging baskets filled with summer flowers, the Sisters and Doña Nicolasa discovered many mutual friends and interests as they conversed. They learned that several people in the neighborhood, refugees like themselves, were from their state of Jalisco.

They all attended Mass the next morning at Holy Innocents, a fifteen-minute walk from the Flores home. Summer's early-morning marine layer of clouds hid the sun, and the brisk ocean breeze filled the air with a briny pungency.

After Mass, they walked back to the house and had a long, leisurely breakfast with the family. In the afternoon, the family took them to the beach.

Doña Nicolasa understood their unspoken need to spend time with God in a beautiful, natural setting. She had made this drive countless times with bishops, priests, and Mexican refugees of all ages, and had seen firsthand the healing of both body and spirit that the ocean brings.

The few hours passed quickly as they walked along the shoreline, breathing in the cool ocean air. Taking off their shoes and stockings, they let the incoming waves wash over their feet and ankles. From time to time, Mother shared her meditative thoughts. "We contemplate the ocean and its vastness, but remember that only God is infinite and immensely beautiful and perfect; someday, the ocean will come to an end."

While taking their final walk along the beach at the end of the day, Mother Luisita motioned for the other two Sisters to come closer.

"I thought about something this afternoon as we were praying in this beautiful place. As I was sitting here, watching the ebb and flow of the waves, I thought about the ups and downs of life, about everything we have been through. See those rocks on the shoreline? As far as we're concerned, we should be like those immovable rocks jutting out into the ocean, so that, when the waves come, they will wash over us, taking away with them all the dust that is on us."

They understood. Taking one long last look at the Pacific Ocean with the sun already fading from view, they meditated quietly on Mother Luisita's words. Afterward, with barely a touch of twilight remaining, they got into the car and returned to their new Long Beach home.

As the days and the weeks passed, their spirits and their ministry began to soar. To be among their own people again gave the Sisters wings. With renewed zeal, now that language was no longer a barrier, they set up programs in Spanish for their Mexican neighbors. To speak openly about God and His love for His people filled them with enthusiasm. The people grew to love them.

During school hours, they began taking the parish census in both Holy Innocents and Our Lady of Mount Carmel, a small mission church about a mile east of Holy Innocents.

Mother Luisita realized that they couldn't remain in the Flores home and expect this wonderful family to support them indefinitely; that would not be just. Father Ott had told them that he would provide a small salary for each Sister, but following the custom in Mexico, Mother Luisita declined his offer. In Mexico, religious communities did not accept stipends or salaries.

Father Ott was well aware that they would soon need a larger house and was already looking for one within the parish boundaries. The best he could find was a good-sized house on Cedar Avenue. It was a little less than a mile from Holy Innocents and just around the corner from Our Lady of Guadalupe, the Mexican mission chapel under Holy Innocents' jurisdiction.

Father Ott came by Doña Nicolasa's home one afternoon to let the Sisters know about the Cedar Avenue house. With Sister Margarita María's assistance, he told Mother Luisita the news. "Mother, I have found a house, but it is badly in need of a thorough cleaning, and the entire interior needs to be painted. I want you all to look at it and let me know what you think about renting it."

That evening, they walked the half mile from the Flores home to the Cedar Avenue house.

It was certainly large enough, but the interior was very dirty.

"Mother, let's take it. Sister Margarita María and I will clean it up and paint it in time for the Sisters' arrival in September," Sister Teresa offered.

"Yes, Mother, please take it. We'll get it fixed up," added Sister Margarita María.

"Yes, Father," said Mother Luisita, "we'll take it if you can help us acquire good cleaning soap, cleaning supplies, interior paint, and brushes."

"All right, Mother. I can do that. When are the new Sisters arriving in Los Angeles?"

"Five more Sisters are arriving on September 12."

Father Ott gave the Sisters cots and bedding as well as the cleaning supplies and paint. From then until September 12, the Sisters worked late into the night, cleaning and painting. As the electricity would not be turned on until the house was occupied, Mother Luisita, night after night, held lighted candles for them as they finished painting the walls and varnishing the floors.

On September 12, Father Ott drove Sister Margarita María and Sister Teresa to pick up the new arrivals at Central Station, and one of the men in the parish drove another car. Mother Luisita waited for them at their house on Cedar Avenue.

Soon the new arrivals — Sister Carmen of Jesus, Sister Elena of the Cross, Sister Josephine of the Child Jesus, Sister María del Refugio of the Sacred Heart, and Sister María del Pilar of the Child Jesus — were on their way to Long Beach. Sister Margarita María leaned over and whispered to Sister Carmen, "Did Ignacio and María De la Torre meet you in Nogales?"

"Yes! What wonderful people they are!"

"Was the tunnel still caved in?"

"Oh, my goodness! Yes! It had rained hard, and so the walk from one train to another was very, very muddy," Sister Carmen answered.

Sister Margarita María ventured a quiet, guarded question. "How are things?"

"Very, very bad." She turned her head away. "I can't talk about it."

They traveled the rest of the way in silence. Sister Margarita María's car arrived at the house first. Sister Elena and Sister Carmen walked up the path and greeted Mother Luisita and kissed her hand, as was the Mexican custom. Both were crying very hard, so Mother tried to distract them. She smiled and said aloud, "Thank You, my Lord. I thank You with all my heart for their safe arrival. Look, my daughters, at our charming little house. Let's go inside. When the others arrive, we will all have something to eat."

As soon as lunch was finished, Sister Elena spoke for all five of them: "Mother, please bear with us. We come with broken hearts. The trip was fine, and we are grateful to be here. It's just that we are overwhelmed right now." She sat back limply like a rag doll.

Mother Luisita looked around the table at each Sister and took a deep breath. "I think it would be a good idea if you take things slowly, one step at a time. We need to build you up more. You will need to rest. As for now, talk to Sister Teresa and Sister Margarita María about whatever you need. Try to rest as best you can. We will wash your clothes for you. Just leave them in the box outside the bathroom. You'll find clean clothes and other items you'll need in your rooms. Take a bath, and if you would like, try to sleep. Sleep as long as you can.

"We have a little oratory where you can go to pray if you like. The Blessed Sacrament is not reserved in our house yet, but the oratory is a peaceful room where you can be alone. If anyone wants to stay and talk, that's fine too, but you look very tired, and my guess is that you probably just need to rest right now."

A few days later, four of the new arrivals were feeling better and smiling more. Mother Luisita took the fifth newcomer,

Sister Refugio, aside, saying, "Come and take a walk with me. Look, my daughter, what a beautiful little house. Did you know Sisters Teresa and Margarita María painted it just for you?" They walked through the various rooms, and then Mother Luisita took her outside.

When they were alone in their backyard, Mother Luisita gently clasped Sister Refugio's hands and said, "My daughter, I brought you here to save your vocation. Our lives as consecrated religious are threatened seriously in Mexico now." Looking off into the distance, she said, "Do you understand? Do you understand what I mean when I say your vocation is at stake?"

Sister Refugio nodded.

Little by little, Sister Refugio's sadness finally began to lessen, and she was able to join the others and help with the catechism classes. She was a teacher par excellence, and being with the children again was the best remedy Mother Luisita could find.

The Sisters' days were very long. They were up at four thirty in the morning and meditation began at five, followed by the chanting of the Little Office of the Blessed Virgin Mary and Holy Mass. After a light breakfast, they left for their various assignments, where they worked until dark. They would come home exhausted and often without having had anything to eat.

They attended Mass six days each week at Our Lady of Guadalupe Mission Chapel. Father Ott was the administrator of this little mission chapel within his parish boundaries, very close to Doña Nicolasa's home, on the same street. Once a week they walked to Our Lady of Mount Carmel for Mass. They split up their work into two groups. One group continued with the census and catechism classes at Holy Innocents and Our Lady of Guadalupe. The recently arrived Sisters took the parish census and held catechism classes at this parish.

IN THE FACE OF DARKNESS

Children were baptized and prepared for their First Communion at both parishes, and numerous adults were prepared for reception of the sacraments. Mother Luisita set up a sewing circle in the garage and answered questions about prayer and Catholic teachings.

Each night, when everyone was in bed, Mother Luisita would slip back into their little oratory and pray.

Lord, we still do not have the Blessed Sacrament here in our little oratory. I miss Your Eucharistic Presence so much. Come, Lord Jesus.

Chapter 18

The Tabernacle

*"The more often you receive Holy Communion, the
more your heart will dilate and the more fervent your
love of God will become, because your relationship
with Him will be all the more intense."*

—From the spiritual notes of Mother Luisita

To be up and about before the sun was nothing new to the Sisters. They woke up to darkness every morning and began their morning prayers well before sunrise.

Mother Luisita was kneeling on the hardwood floor with her hands placed modestly under her brown scapular. Her eyes were closed, and her lips were moving ever so slightly in prayer.

Lord, we have no income. Please help us now. How do You want us to support ourselves? Most Sacred Heart of Jesus, I place my trust in You.

The two hundred dollars in gold coins that Mother Luisita had brought from Mexico were almost gone. Occasionally the Sisters received small donations, but these would not sustain them. The eight Sisters lived in extreme poverty, with only the barest necessities. They walked everywhere, because even bus fare was too expensive. When their leather shoes wore out and could no longer be patched, they purchased tennis shoes at fifty cents a pair.

"Let us all place ourselves in the hands of God," Mother Luisita told the other Sisters, "so that He will do whatever He pleases with us, and let us wish nothing except what He wishes."

Father Ott had been concerned for some time about how these dear women were able to manage without any income. He observed the poverty in which they lived and inquired several times about this. When he offered again to pay a small salary to each of the Sisters working in the parish, Mother Luisita replied kindly, but firmly, "We never charge to teach the word of God."

Father Ott finally decided to share the dire finances of the Carmelite refugees with his parishioners one Sunday at Mass. The people were not wealthy, but they gave what they could, and enough money was collected to sustain the refugees for a while. After Father Ott's appeal, donations would appear from time to time at the house on Cedar Street. And, on their part, the Sisters learned how to prepare simple meals using fruit and vegetables that were unknown in Mexico.

Sister Margarita María approached Mother Luisita one afternoon when they were alone in the house. "Mother, so many people are asking us for holy cards and rosaries that I would like your permission to open a small store in a corner of the front room of our house."

"To have a store in the same house where we are living—do you think that's wise?" She knitted her brows in concern.

"Yes, Mother. There is no other place to put it. I think that it would benefit our neighbors as well as us. They will receive the items they request, and we'll make some money to help us survive here."

"All right, then. Go ahead and try it, and if you can find some place away from the house, it would be even better."

"God reward you, Mother. Remember, I did have some training in business!" Her eyes sparkled. Sister Margarita María thrived on challenges.

The little store was a success. By saving a little each week, Sister Margarita María soon added prayer books and small statues to her tiny inventory and then decided to include used clothing. When the parishioners heard about the store, they cleaned out their closets and donated used clothing to help the Sisters' business venture. By word of mouth, the news spread quickly that the Carmelites had the best used clothing in town, for the best price — almost nothing. Refugees like themselves were ecstatic to acquire more clothing. They, too, had fled Mexico with barely more than the clothes on their backs.

Yes, the store was an excellent suggestion. We need that income.

When the store was up and running, Sister Margarita María asked for permission to teach some Spanish to adults in the parish. Father Ott sent his associate pastor, Father Dillon, and five women to be her first pupils. Each lesson cost fifty cents per person. The Spanish lessons proved to be a financial godsend. Every cent mattered.

"Do you have a moment to speak with us, Father?" Mother Luisita and Sister Margarita María asked Father Ott one day after Mass.

"Certainly."

Mother spoke, and Sister Margarita María translated her request to have a chapel in their house with an altar and a tabernacle. She humbly inquired if they could reserve the Blessed Sacrament in their home, which was serving as a convent.

IN THE FACE OF DARKNESS

I wish with all my heart I could speak English fluently. Dear Lord, please give Sister Margarita María the right words.

Finally, Father Ott said, "No. I'm sorry, Sisters. We just can't afford it at this time. Sister Margarita María, tell Mother Luisita that Holy Innocents is a new parish. It began only a few years ago with only thirty families. Our parish finances are very low."

As he was leaving, he turned back toward the Sisters.

"Mother, I almost forgot to give you something." Father Ott took a folded paper out of his pocket. He carefully unfolded it, smoothed it out, and gave it to Mother Luisita. "A priest I know gave me this yesterday. It is a newspaper article with a photograph of a Sister at the Hospital of the Sacred Heart in Atotonilco. Isn't that your hospital? She isn't wearing a habit, but she is wearing a short veil to hold her hair back. Is she one of your Sisters?"

She looked carefully at the paper. "Yes, oh yes, that's Sister María del Rosario." Handing the paper to Sister Margarita María, she asked, "What did it say?"

Sister Margarita María took a moment to read the article. "Mother, it says that a wave of death is spreading over Atotonilco from a smallpox epidemic that is a consequence of the uprising. So many unclaimed corpses are lying in the streets, and so many wounded have been left unattended. It also says that the victims are all being taken to the Hospital of the Sacred Heart where the very few doctors and nurses are working day and night to help the patients."

"They are heroines; my daughters are heroines," Mother said as she passed the newspaper clipping to Sister Teresa.

Sister Teresa stared at the photo. "Mother, look how thin she is. Just look closely."

Father Ott cleared his throat. "Excuse me, Sisters, please keep this article. It is part of your history."

"Thank you, Father. May God reward you. We are very grateful."

There was a hint of autumn in the air as the Sisters walked back to the house. Trees lining the road showed the barest tinge of their fall colors. Seasonal changes were beginning—the whisper of the morning breeze through the leaves, the reappearance of the morning fog rolling back to the ocean, the quiet of the neighborhood, where children who had recently played early-morning hopscotch had already begun their school day. Mother Luisita walked home in a meditative frame of mind and remained quiet most of the day.

That evening Mother Luisita called the seven Sisters together and showed everyone the newspaper clipping. The recently arrived Sisters knew the story of the clipping. They pieced together what they remembered as each took her turn relating the parts of the story she recalled.

Sister Carmen, who was still holding the clipping, spoke first. "Mother, after the reconcentration order was issued, a horde of people descended into our little town. They were mostly from the ranches in Los Altos. Hundreds, maybe thousands, I don't know the actual number. Too many, for sure."

"Atotonilco became overpopulated," Sister Refugio continued. "More and more of the wounded were brought to our little hospital, and very soon we experienced a shortage of food. All of these factors caused the outbreak of a smallpox epidemic. Our nursing Sisters told us that working conditions were unbearable as they treated all three forms of the terrible disease—confluent, black, and, in many of the patients, madness. The federal troops also brought their wounded to us. The soldiers brought some field tents that were intended for about 30 patients, but we ended up cramming up to 105 plague victims in them."

IN THE FACE OF DARKNESS

Sister María del Pilar spoke next: "Mother, our nursing Sisters told us that the condition of their infected bodies was beyond description, and there was an unbearable stench within the tents because of the overcrowding. One sick woman was not able to sit up to take the nourishment she needed. Sister María del Rosario asked, 'May I help you?' Without waiting for an answer, she assisted the woman. She continued to support her until she had finished the meal. She was unaware that the doctors and everyone present were greatly edified by her charity."

Sister Carmen continued: "Each day, reporters from Guadalajara would rush to the hospital to get their daily updates on the epidemic. One of the reporters took Sister María del Rosario's picture after he had noticed her self-sacrifice and courage. The photo was released both in the Mexican press and in newspapers across the border. That's the story, Mother, unless anyone knows some more facts."

"I will keep this newspaper clipping. I think it deserves to be seen by future Sisters. It defines who we are. It is pure charity.

"I have other news that I want to share with all of you tonight," Mother Luisita continued. "My daughters, we have now been in California for almost four months, working at Holy Innocents, Mount Carmel, and Our Lady of Guadalupe Mission. We have our house and our little store. Sister Margarita María is giving Spanish lessons. We are preparing for several more Sisters to come as soon as possible, but, Sisters, that which we need the most is still missing—our own little chapel with the Blessed Sacrament right here in our house." She looked intently at her Carmelite Sisters, who waited expectantly to hear what was coming next.

After a short pause, Mother continued. "Sister Margarita María and I asked Father Ott today if we could have the Blessed Sacrament reserved in our oratory, and he told us that he doesn't have enough money to fulfill the requirements for the reservation of the Blessed Sacrament. He doesn't even have funds for an altar and a tabernacle. The requirements to have the Blessed Sacrament reserved, even in the smallest of chapels, state that the Blessed Sacrament must be enclosed in a tabernacle affixed to an altar. Father Ott said we were asking for a miracle.

"Sisters, he reminded me that all the parishes near us are new parishes, established only a few years ago, and are low on finances also. He told me that Holy Innocents has just over thirty families and Our Lady of Guadalupe has about a hundred families, mostly Mexican refugees like us. So I have been praying about this all day, and here is what I'd like to do."

She turned toward Sister Teresa.

"Sister Teresa, will you kindly bring me the brown doctor's bag that I carried from Mexico? I left it in the oratory."

They waited in silence while Sister Teresa went to get the bag. When she returned, Mother Luisita asked, "Would you put it down on this table?" She pointed to a small end table. Then Mother made the Sign of the Cross with great devotion and knelt on the wooden floor next to the table. The other Sisters looked at each other, and then, one by one, they also knelt, wondering what was happening. Mother opened the bag and reverently removed a small bundle and placed it on the table.

"Sisters, remember when we were without Mass and deprived of Communion for such a long time in Mexico?"

They nodded. How could they forget?

"Remember that we were given permission to keep a small, wooden tabernacle and a little ciborium with us?"

They nodded again.

"Sisters, I brought them with me on the train. I asked our Blessed Mother to protect them so they wouldn't be taken from us."

She carefully unfolded the covering; reverently removed the small, highly polished wooden tabernacle; and placed it on top of the fabric. It was about seven inches wide, nine inches high, and about five inches deep. Then she produced a little key and opened the simple, wooden door and removed an even smaller ciborium.

"Mother, we didn't know you brought these with you!" All seven Sisters were astonished. They knew of Mother's custom of bringing a tabernacle to the opening of each new foundation of her community. They had witnessed her invitation to Our Lord, asking Him to come and dwell within each tabernacle. But they had no idea she had continued this practice on her dangerous journey to Los Angeles.

"Yes, I did. I brought our tabernacle and ciborium with us even though it was so very risky. Sisters, I would like to propose to all of you that we begin nine days of a prayer to Saint Thérèse. We have just enough time to complete the novena before her feast day. I would like to propose that all eight of us join together in fervent prayer, asking through her intercession that we may obtain funds for an altar and a tabernacle. Will you do this with me?"

In almost perfect unison, all seven Sisters responded, "Yes!"

"All right. I'm going to leave this tiny tabernacle right here on the table with the door open as an invitation to Our Lord to come and enter."[19]

---

[19] Sister Piedad Arquieta, O.C.D., interview with the author, Alhambra, California, November 12, 1997. Note: In addition to the interview with Sister Piedad Arquieta, Sister Teresa Navarro in her personal testimony wrote: "We wanted the Blessed Sacrament in the house. We had a tabernacle we had brought with us from Mexico. Father Ott said we were asking for a miracle. Mother Luisita told us to set up a table and the tabernacle.

The Tabernacle

∞

A few days later, Father Ott visited the Sisters and brought his mother along so she could meet them. The Sisters practiced the variety of English greetings they had just learned from Sister Margarita María.

"You have no idea how very much we are indebted to your son, Mrs. Ott. He is our guardian angel here in the United States. We are all so very grateful to him," said Sister Margarita María.

Mary Ott smiled as she listened to Sister Margarita María, who obviously knew more English than the others. She turned to look at her son with obvious pride.

As Sister Margarita María translated during a lively conversation with his mother, Father Ott began to take a good look at the interior of the living room. He noted the store and the lift the room had received with the new paint. As his eyes panned the rest of the room, he saw the little table with the small, wooden tabernacle. He turned toward Mother Luisita, pointed at the tabernacle, and asked, "Mother, what is that?"

Some days later, Father Ott arrived with his mother so that we could meet her and greet her. He spoke a little Spanish."

Author's note: I took Sister Teresa's words to mean that the tabernacle was brought by Mother Luisita, Sister Margarita María, and Sister Teresa Navarro in June 1927. Another possibility would be that the second group of refugees, who arrived in the United States in September 1927, could have brought the little tabernacle. The oral tradition of our community and the tribunal testimony of Sister Ines of Jesus affirm that Mother Luisita brought a tabernacle to the new foundations. "The criterion Mother Luisita followed for the new foundations was wholly apostolic, and there had to be a new tabernacle where Jesus in the Blessed Sacrament could be adored, and a place where the poor could be served," said Sister Ines of Jesus.

IN THE FACE OF DARKNESS

Sister Margarita María told him about the persecution, being without Mass for so many months, the risk Mother had taken in bringing it with her on the train and their nine-day novena to Saint Thérèse. He was deeply moved. He, too, had a personal devotion to this young Carmelite who had been proclaimed a saint only two years before. He remained thoughtful for over a minute.

"My dear Sisters," Father Ott finally began with the help of Sister Margarita María, "it seems that Saint Thérèse, the Little Flower, loves you very much. An elderly gentleman of our parish recently died and left one hundred dollars to be used for a charitable cause within our parish. It is enough for a tabernacle and an altar. Sisters, you will soon have the Blessed Sacrament here with you at this convent. Mother, I'll bring you a catalog tomorrow."

That night, Mother Luisita told the Sisters, "We will go ahead and finish our novena, but instead of asking Saint Thérèse, we will thank her."

Father Ott saw to it that an altar was made, and then the Sisters waited over a month for the tabernacle to arrive. Both were placed in the oratory during the first week in November. Father Ott celebrated the first Mass in the little chapel on November 4, 1927, the first Friday of the month. It was offered for the repose of the soul of the kind benefactor who had bequeathed the hundred dollars to Father Ott.

In the meantime, Father Callahan had kept in touch with Mother Luisita regarding kinds of work for the refugees. He told her that the Christian Brothers were building a new college in Moraga, California, and were looking for a community of Sisters to do domestic work. In a few weeks, he would have more information, but he wanted Mother to have the time to think about it and pray over it. Perhaps this invitation would be an answer to her prayers.

A few days later, Mother Luisita became ill with bronchitis, and the Sisters tried to figure out what to do.

"How can we get enough money to buy Mother what she needs?" asked Sister Margarita María.

Sister Teresa raised her hand. "Leave it to me. We'll have the money soon." She walked into the next room, confidently brought back a little basket, and hung it on their small statue of Saint Joseph. Then she knelt down and made the Sign of the Cross. "Saint Joseph, here I am again, asking your help. Mother Luisita is very sick, and we don't have any money to buy her the proper medicine and nourishment. Please leave some money in the basket or show us where we can get some. Thank you, dear Saint Joseph. You have helped me every time I have asked. Please help us now.

"Don't worry, Sisters. Just you wait and see how Saint Joseph will bring the money to us."

One morning, not long after she had placed the basket on the statue, Sister Teresa was burning the trash when a car drove up slowly and then stopped. A man got out of the car and gave her ten dollars as a donation. It was just enough for Mother's nourishment and medicine. After that, more people started giving them donations. Sister Teresa dutifully returned to her little statue.

"Thank you very much, Saint Joseph." She thought a moment and then turned toward the others. "Shall I just leave the basket hanging there?" Before they could respond, she answered her own question: "I'd better take it off. We don't want to be greedy."

Chapter 19

Christmas in Long Beach

*Remain very serene while awaiting God's will. In the
meantime, be at peace, placing yourself into the hands
of God and offering acts of confidence in His Divine
Majesty. Be like a servant watching for the master to
make known his desires in order to carry them out.*

—Undated letter of Mother Luisita to Sister
Socorro during the religious persecution

November passed into December, and soon it was the holy season
of Advent. Each Sister prepared for the coming of Christmas,
and to these Carmelites, that preparation was far more spiritual
than material. In Mexico, every year, the children would send
letters to the Child Jesus with their requests for gifts, and then
the Christ Child would bring their gifts with the Magi on January
6, the solemnity of the Epiphany.

Nine days before Christmas, the celebration of Las Posadas
began. So many people offered to help.

"I'll make Mary's dress."

"Our family will make Joseph's clothes."

"My father will play the guitar."

On and on it went, until everything was ready. A young couple took the roles of Mary and Joseph. Parents dressed their children as shepherds, and each night, the people processed to a different home while praying the Rosary and singing the traditional hymns.

Saint Joseph, staff in hand, asked for lodging in a different home for eight consecutive nights. Mary entered each home with him. Prayers, refreshments, and a colorful piñata filled with candies hung from a conspicuous place in the living room or whatever space the family was able to provide. Each child tried to hit the piñata with a stick while blindfolded until someone finally cracked it open with a good whack and candies fell out upon the floor.

Each night seemed to become colder than the previous evening as winter descended upon Long Beach. As they slowly wound their way around the neighborhood, holding lighted candles, the Sisters found themselves breathing into their hands in an attempt to warm them. They felt their faces become numb, and they tried to recall the warmth of the summer sun during their first weeks in Long Beach.

On December twenty-first, all bundled up because of the cold, Mother Luisita sat huddled in a corner of the kitchen and began writing a letter to Father José Refugio Huerta, a friend from Guadalajara who had also escaped the persecution and was now living in Los Angeles. She knew the Huerta family well. There were four brothers. Ezekiel and Salvador had been martyred on April 3, 1927, in Jalisco, just a few months before the Carmelite Sisters had escaped from Guadalajara. After brutal torture, these heroic laymen died without ever revealing the whereabouts of their priest brothers. Nor did they reveal the names or hiding places of any of the other priests or Cristeros.

Mother Luisita weighed the pros and cons of accepting the invitation for the Sisters to do domestic work in Moraga. She couldn't decide.

Should I stay here or return to Mexico? I need clarity. Should I follow up with the opportunity to work in Moraga with the Christian Brothers? I don't know. I just don't know. Maybe the next group of Sisters could travel straight from Mexico to Moraga? I'll ask Father José's advice.

She wrote the letter right away with trust in the advice of Father José Refugio.

A few days before Christmas, Father Ott gave the Sisters a small Christmas tree, some ornaments, and an inexpensive nativity set for their home. "You are going to be receiving gifts, and our custom is to leave them all wrapped up under the Christmas tree until Christmas," he told them. "Or you could open them on Christmas Eve, after Midnight Mass, as some families do."

He was right. Brightly wrapped gifts began arriving, and the Sisters dutifully placed them under their little Christmas tree. They also received Christmas cards, another new custom for them. On Christmas Eve, more and more people came to the house bringing gifts, whatever they could afford. It was difficult to keep the traditional Carmelite prayerful silence in preparation for the solemnity of Christmas.

Right before Midnight Mass on Christmas Eve, the final Posada procession ended at the church, and everyone waited with hushed expectation for the Mass to begin. The altar servers entered with lit candles, the choir sang Christmas carols, and

IN THE FACE OF DARKNESS

Father Ott walked up the aisle carrying the statue of the Christ Child. At the stroke of midnight, he placed the statue of the Divine Infant in the manger of the large nativity set that had been set up on the side altar. The refugees in the church had never been poorer than on that first Christmas in California. They knew that they would have very little to eat the next day, but it didn't matter.

They were free.

Early Christmas morning, the Carmelites were awakened by a loud pounding on the front door that reminded them too much of the persecution they had experienced. "What's happening?" Their knees were knocking. A few minutes later, singing could be heard coming from the front porch of their home. Sister Margarita María pulled the curtain back ever so slightly, just enough to peek out, and she saw a line of men standing in front of their house singing Christmas carols. They sang a few more carols and then left.

After the men walked away, Sister Margarita María cautiously opened the front door and found a large basket with a huge red bow. She tried to pick it up, but it was too heavy.

"Sisters, will some of you help me pick up this big basket, please?"

They brought it inside. When Mother Luisita removed the bow, they discovered to their amazement an assortment of fresh fruit and vegetables, a large turkey, fresh bread, and all the traditional Christmas dinner ingredients. Candy and other desserts were also included. The Sisters found a card inside that read, "Merry Christmas from the B.P.O.E."

Mother Luisita looked at the group and said, "Sisters, we need to find out what this B.P.O.E. stands for so we can thank them. B.P.O.E. How curious!"

Later that afternoon, as Mother Luisita glanced around the table at the Christmas dinner provided by the B.P.O.E., she noticed the laughter. The Sisters were smiling and laughing together.

She couldn't have asked for a better gift.

The de la Peña family in 1896 following the death of Dr.
Pascual Rojas. Luisita, a widow, is seated in the middle row,
first person from left, next to her mother, Luisa de la Peña.

In 1904, Mother Luisita entered the Monastery of Saint Teresa in
Guadalajara. The custom of this cloistered Discalced Carmelite
community was to take a photo in the Carmelite habit prior to
entrance. Mother Luisita is thirty-eight years of age in this picture.

The first novices of Mother Luisita's new community in 1923. Seated in the center is Mother Isabel Rioseco, a Franciscan Sister of Our Lady of Refuge, who was sent by the archbishop to teach the first novices.

Mother Luisita is seated in the front row with two children, her first companions, and some patients at the Hospital del Sagrado Corazón in 1904 in Atotonilco.

Left: Doña Nicolasa Flores, who opened her Long Beach home to Mexican refugees, including the Carmelites. Right: Mother Luisita and Sister Margarita María at Santa Teresita Rest Home (ca. 1936).

Father Leroy S. Callahan.   Monsignor Francis Ott.

Top: Father Leroy S. Callahan with Sisters and the Juventud
Católica Femenina Mexicana at Saint Patrick's (1929);
bottom: Holy Innocents Church, Long Beach (ca. 1940).

Top: Archbishop Francisco Orozco y Jiménez with Sisters (Mother
Luisita is to his right; ca. 1936); bottom: Santa Teresita Rest Home.

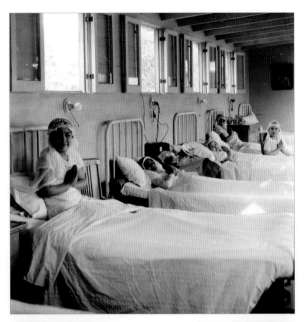

Top: Tuberculosis patients at Santa Teresita Rest Home (1930s); bottom: Santa Teresita patients sewing a quilt.

The six sides of the urn containing Mother Luisita's
remains show the elements of her charism.

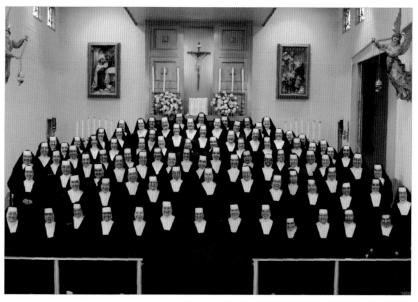

The Carmelite Sisters of the Most Sacred Heart of Los Angeles today.

Superiors General of Mother Luisita's two communities
(2016). Left: Mother Judith Zúniga, O.C.D., Superior
General of the Carmelite Sisters of the Most Sacred Heart
of Los Angeles; right: Mother Maria Elena Pacheco, C.S.C.,
Superior General of Carmelitas del Sagrado Corazón.

Sisters from Mother Luisita's two communities break bread
together on the 150th anniversary of her birth (2016).

Chapter 20

Discerning God's Will

We do what we need to do, not what we want to do.

—Undated letter of Mother Luisita to Sister Teresita

After an early morning Mass on December 26, Mother Luisita handed Father Ott the card with the B.P.O.E. signature. "Father, what does this mean? Who is this?" She was able to ask her question herself, without an interpreter.

"This is a gift for you from the local Elks' Club, Mother," Father Ott said. "They give out Christmas baskets to people in need every year." He turned the card over, looking at it more closely. "I'm glad they found you. They helped many, many refugee families this year. The initials of their organization stand for the Benevolent and Protective Order of Elks."

After Sister Margarita María translated, Mother made a mental note to send them a thank-you card right away and also to thank them in person if the opportunity arose. Later that morning, continuing her custom of trying to answer at least one letter a day, Mother Luisita sat down at a little table, opened the doctor's bag, and took out her pile of letters. Several Sisters had written to her, and she wanted to answer them. She continued to use code words and to sign each letter with one of her aliases.

IN THE FACE OF DARKNESS

The persecution was at its zenith. Many of the Sisters wrote of the deprivations that continued to multiply. Mother Luisita had a word for each.

In replying to one letter, she wrote, "There can be storms in our souls more terrible than those at sea, but we were told not to fear because God Our Lord is with us. In His own time, He will calm the storm, and we will be safe and have peace."

She tried to alleviate the suffering she saw in every line of another letter. "The things that you describe in your letter that are happening now have always happened. They are like waves of the sea that are suddenly falling on top of the world, and then everything appears as if we're at the end, but it's not so. These things pass like a strong storm that, in a way, is beneficial to clean the atmosphere."

When she was finished, she held the pen with both hands, rolling it back and forth as she thought. Finally, she put it down and began to pray.

My Lord, I hesitate to accept the invitation to work at the new college in Moraga. Please don't get me wrong, Lord. I'm not afraid of hard work. What is Your will for us, Lord? Please let me know before I sign any contract. Is this Your will for us?

She left the unanswered letters on the table and went to the chapel to discern before the Blessed Sacrament what would be best for the community. That evening after dinner, she called the Sisters into the living room.

"There's something I've been meaning to share with you. Now that we've been here almost six months, Father Callahan spoke with me about finding work for the other Sisters who will be coming. He told me that the Christian Brothers at Saint Mary's College in Moraga, California, have an opening at the new college they are constructing. This means that in the near future they will need a community of Sisters to help with the domestic work. One of the Brothers is going to write a letter to us soon, giving us more details. Archbishop Hanna of San Francisco told Bishop Cantwell, who told Father Callahan, who is now asking us if we would like to accept this position."

She shifted in her chair uneasily. Clearly this possibility had unsettled her. Bringing both hands to her forehead, she pressed her fingers against her temples as she thought.

After remaining in this position for a few minutes, she clasped her hands together and told the group, "Let us pray about this. I'm just not sure if this is the right move for us. I wrote Father José Refugio Huerta and asked his advice. He hasn't answered yet. The move to Moraga would provide work for us that will not require much English, and we could bring twenty more Sisters from Mexico, but I'm not sure if it is God's will. I'll let you know more after the letter arrives from the Christian Brothers."

She took a moment to glance at the Sisters. They looked happy and at peace.

I can't wait to bring as many of our Sisters to Los Angeles as possible. Yes, as many as possible.

Standing up, she addressed the group. "And I think you'll like my next surprise for all of you! I've finalized the arrangements for the next group of Sisters to arrive in just twelve weeks, on March 25, the solemnity of the Annunciation. Here is another prayer intention for us. We need to find a bigger house. Let's join in prayer, asking Our Lord to show us His will in both these matters."

That night, she knelt close to the tabernacle. Riveting her eyes on the tabernacle, she poured out her heart in prayer.

Lord, I don't want to bother You over and over again, but I forgot to mention our need for a bigger house. Thank You, my Lord, for

*taking care of us. Please send us a larger house as soon as possible.
And I thank You ahead of time!*

∞

About a week later, Father Huerta answered Mother's letter.

December 30, 1927
Rev. José Refugio Huerta
Los Angeles, California

Reverend Mother Luisa Josefa of the Most Blessed
Sacrament,

... Regarding the coming of the rest of the Sisters, it
seems to me that what you should do is to request Bishop
Hanna of San Francisco to permit you to bring them here,
explaining their circumstances and the need to bring them
here without causing a hardship to anyone.

In reference to the difficulties pertaining to the goods
of the community, do not worry. Have confidence in God,
Who is our Father, and Who does not cease to watch over
them, and Who will not allow more than what is within
His goodness and for our well-being. Be then trusting
and at peace.

I promised the Sisters I would go there, but it was not
possible. God willing, I will go soon.

May God keep you well and in His grace.

Attentively, your servant in Christ,
J.R. Huerta

The following day, the letter from Brother Joseph of the Christian Brothers arrived.

"Sisters," announced Mother Luisita, "the letter from Moraga arrived. It says Bishop Cantwell recommends that some of us move to Moraga in order to help the Christian Brothers at their college. Father Huerta also advises that we should go to Moraga. It's time to decide whether we should go and do domestic work, as an exception, because it is certainly not one of the apostolates outlined in our constitutions."

Letters went back and forth from Moraga to Long Beach. Different parts of the contract were explained more thoroughly. Then, at the beginning of January, a letter from Father Pedro finally arrived. He was in the United States because of the persecution in Mexico and with the hope of establishing a foundation of Discalced Carmelite Friars in the United States. He wrote that he had already contacted the Archdiocese of San Francisco and was not accepted there and was currently in Arizona, hoping a diocese would accept their community.

Meanwhile, Father Ott was well aware that the Sisters would need a larger house by March 25, when the next group of Sisters would arrive. He had looked and looked but couldn't find an affordable house within the parish boundaries. All during February, he searched for the right house for the Sisters. One morning, as he was leaving the chapel of Our Lady of Guadalupe, he noticed a large house being moved onto an empty lot only a few yards from the chapel. It would be an ideal house and location for the Sisters, he thought, and he sought out the owner of the lot.

"Would you like me to take you through the house, Father?" the owner asked.

"Yes, thank you."

As the two men walked through the large residence, Father Ott was quite sure he would not be able to afford it.

"How much is the rent?" he asked the owner. "I don't think I could afford any more than I'm paying now."

"How much are you paying now?" the owner answered.

Father Ott told him.

The neighbor took off his hat and scratched his head. He looked at Father and then back at the house several times, as if he were a spectator at a ping-pong match. Then he scratched his head again, looked up, and said, "All right, you can have it. I'm not Catholic myself. I'm Protestant, but I've seen the Sisters as they walk by on their way to the mission, and they impress me. Anyway, it's all for a good cause, isn't it?"

Father Ott nodded.

He had just witnessed a miracle.

Chapter 21

Decisions, Decisions

*Let us bless Our Lord for everything. He allows
only what is best for us. Let us go forward, good
seamen, for our Love is waiting on the seashore.*

—Letter to Mother Elena, 1934

January 1928 was cold, very cold. The same ocean breeze that
refreshed the Sisters when they had first arrived now chilled
them. Although they piled on extra clothing, they continued to
shiver. Conserving every cent, they had no heat in their home.
Father Ott told the Sisters their new home would be on Chestnut Avenue near Our Lady of Guadalupe. "Sisters, this time we
aren't renting a house for you. Instead, I purchased the house,
and as soon as escrow goes through, I'll let you know and you
can all move in."

The Sisters braced themselves for another house without heat
in the damp, coastal city. New physical ailments had plagued
Mother Luisita ever since she came to the United States. She had
found out that she had diabetes and that her kidney condition
was becoming chronic. A heart condition was also developing.

"My albumin is high again, Sisters. The doctor told me that
is why I feel so cold. Don't worry. I'll just bundle up."

"Sometimes I feel quite sick," she confided to them, "and only God knows how I'm going to tolerate the winter, but I also know that it will never be more than what Our Lord permits. He wants only what is best for us, because He loves us so much."

As donations came in for their secondhand clothing store, the Sisters searched through the piles to find warm, woolen sweaters, stockings, jackets, or coats that Mother could wear to alleviate her distress. Mother Luisita described herself as "all bundled up and looking like a wrapped-up tamale."

By February 18, she had made her decision. She would move a large number of Sisters to Moraga. Picking up her pen, she began to write. She gave the draft to Sister Margarita María, who translated it into English.

February 18, 1928

Dear Brother Joseph,

I look forward to meeting you in a few weeks so we can talk through the specific points of the contract. I think we would be able to commit to two years, and then we can decide at that time if we will remain at Saint Mary's or return to Los Angeles.

On behalf of all of the Sisters, thank you for the invitation to join the domestic service staff of Saint Mary's College.

We pray that the construction is going well and on schedule.

Sincerely yours in Christ,
Sister María Luisa Josefa of the Most Blessed Sacrament

Several days later, Father Ott came by to see the refugees and told them, "Escrow closed today. Mother, you can move in anytime you want." During that week and the next, little by little, they moved into the new house. As the younger Sisters did most of the heavier work, Mother Luisita used the time to answer a few more letters. They were piling up fast.

Her first letter was to a Sister suffering from anxiety and discouragement. "May your life be filled with blessings. May they, like the valuable rain, help the seeds of those virtues most pleasing to God Our Lord to germinate within your soul, embellishing it with virtue."

To another, she wrote about the stately cypress tree outside their house in Atotonilco. "Our soul should be like that cypress, always pointing to heaven. We have to cling to Our Lord to be able to have life, just as the branches in the trees have to be attached to the trunk to receive the sap."

"Mother, we've finished transporting the smaller items from the Cedar house to our new Chestnut Avenue home. Father Ott said the men will come by within the hour to move the altar and the tabernacle."

Sister Refugio glanced at Mother Luisita. "Mother, are you all right? Do you need any help?" Sister Refugio was almost herself again—generous, outgoing, and practical.

"No, thank you. I'm just writing a few letters. If you have time, will you give the new chapel one more dusting and one more mopping so it will be extra clean when the Blessed Sacrament arrives?"

"Surely, Mother. I'm on my way now."

By nightfall, the move to the new house was completed, and the best part was still to come. Father Ott had arranged that one of the priests would arrive at their new house every morning to celebrate Mass in their own little chapel. Tomorrow would be the first Mass. So much to be thankful for!

IN THE FACE OF DARKNESS

One morning, a few days after they had moved in, the Sisters were in their little chapel waiting for the priest to arrive for morning Mass. They waited and waited, but he never came. Not having a telephone, and with no way to contact him to see what happened, Mother Luisita decided that they would all walk to Mass at Our Lady of Guadalupe Mission.

When the Mass was over and they were leaving, a couple approached them. "Sisters, I'm Peter O'Donnell, and this is my wife, Julia. May I ask what order you belong to?"

Sister Margarita María answered. "We're Carmelite Sisters from Mexico working here in the United States as refugees from religious persecution there. We teach catechism in three parishes and are also taking the parish census."

Mr. O'Donnell was drawn to help these Sisters in some way. "Sisters, will you accept a small donation?"

"Yes, certainly, and God bless you."

He took out a pen and his checkbook, wrote in the amount, and gave the paper to Mother Luisita.

"God reward you, Mr. O'Donnell."

Mother Luisita folded the check in half and didn't look at the amount until she got home. It was made out to the Carmelite Sisters for fifty dollars. She laid it on the table next to the bill she had been given earlier that morning from the milkman with his note: "Dear Sisters, this will be your last delivery of milk pending your payment indicated here."

She looked at the milk bill of almost fifty dollars. Now, thanks to God's providence and the O'Donnells' generosity, they could pay this bill.

Thank You, my dearest Lord. I praise Your gracious and bountiful providence and ask You to please send special blessings to this couple who helped us pay our milk bill.

That night, when the Sisters were relaxing together after dinner, they once again caught a glimpse of the fire emanating from the soul of Mother Luisita. She had closed her eyes and was praying.

Thank You, Lord, that we had to attend our Mass today at Our Lady of Guadalupe. Thank You, Lord!

Chapter 22

Oakland

To be submissive to the adorable will of
God: that is enough to be at peace.

—Letter to Sister Socorro, 1832

Everything fell into place. Eight Sisters arrived on March 25, and five arrived in May. It was definitely the right time to make the necessary move to Moraga, California. They had to move. There would be more than thirty Sisters in the United States by August.

Kneeling before the Blessed Sacrament, immersed in prayer, Mother Luisita's radiant face reflected her intimate relationship with her Beloved.

My Lord, I don't know how to thank You for working this huge miracle for me. I believed. I trusted. Lord, I knew You could do this for us, and I come today to thank You with all my heart and soul. You gave all of us passports, Lord—all of us. I always tell the Sisters, "Let God do His part." And each time You do this for us, I am so deeply affected by Your sovereign power and boundless mercy. Jesus, I thank You again with all my heart. Yes, Your mercies never fail. They are new every morning; great is Your faithfulness.[20]

[20] See Lamentations 3:23–24.

Later that week, she met with Sister Carmen and Sister Margarita María.

"Sisters, I would like the two of you to travel to Moraga ahead of the rest of us—let's say about a week ahead of the others—to find out more about Saint Mary's."

Before they answered, Mother saw a little hesitancy.

Who could blame them? Alone in a strange country, separated from the rest of us.

Just as Mother Luisita was about to encourage them, the two Sisters looked at each other, smiled, and answered together, "Yes, Mother, we'll go."

It took courage for them to make the trip to Oakland. Each Sister had butterflies in her stomach, and the journey would be so much more than a trip to another city. It would be a journey in faith: so many unknowns, so little money, so few friends. They would have considered it an adventure if it were not for their real fear of the unknown, which was uppermost in their minds. It is interesting how faith can coexist with fear, they thought.

At the beginning of May, Sister Margarita María and Sister Carmen traveled by train to San Francisco and then by boat for the seven-mile crossing to Oakland.

They were met in Oakland by two Christian Brothers, who accompanied them to Oakland's Providence Hospital, across the street from the Christian Brothers' Saint Mary's College High School.

"That was our school until recently," one of the Brothers explained, pointing to the campus across the street. The students had nicknamed it "the Brickpile." It's no longer in use because the high school has moved to Berkeley and the college is in the process of transferring to Moraga, where a new college is still under construction. We've just about emptied out the entire campus, and that is why we've planned for your accommodations with the Sisters who run Providence Hospital, where we are now."

San Francisco's Catholic newspaper, *The Monitor*, took a special interest in "the exiled nuns of the Little Flower from Mexico," as they named the Carmelite refugees. Fred Williams, one of their best journalists, interviewed the two Carmelites at the hospital, where they would stay until the construction of the college would be completed. From the very beginning, the Sisters found a friend in this intuitive and empathetic journalist.

"Sisters, it was an honor and privilege to meet you today," Fred Williams remarked following their interview, as he began packing up his materials. "I'll be back. I am very interested in following your story and writing some follow-up articles from time to time."

The article was published on May 12, 1928. As soon as it arrived, Sister Margarita María read it aloud to Sister Carmen, stopping to translate every few phrases.

CARMELITES GRATEFUL FOR ST. MARY'S OFFER
by Fred W. Williams
May 12, 1928

Quietly Brother Gregory, provincial of the Christian Brothers from St. Mary's, led the interviewer down the cool, dark hallways of Providence Hospital in Oakland. At the door to an ante-room, he stopped and raised his hand in gesture not unlike a Benediction. "They are here, by the window," he said. "The Carmelites of Mexico." You may talk to them.

By a window sat two women in coarse robes of brown, a young woman and an old woman with hands clasped and eyes lowered.

Two little Carmelite nuns exiled in a strange land. At sight of Brother Gregory, they rose and smiled, and Brother Gregory introduced them. The younger nun, scarcely more than a girl she seemed, was Sister Margarita María. The other one was Sister Carmen.

Sister Margarita María looked not unlike the pictures of her own Little Flower. Sister Carmen's face was worn and strained. Sister Margarita María, speaking excellent English, told their story.

Yes, they were Carmelites and exiles. It had been very hard to be driven by soldiers from their house of God, driven into the streets and to have their habits stripped from them by rude men, and forced to seek refuge among friends, singly, hiding like criminals from the law....

Sister Margarita María's voice lowered to a whisper. "Ah, the men and the boys of the Faith in Mexico. They were butchered and shot. Their tongues were cut out when they cried, 'Long live Christ the King,' but they died gloriously, martyrs of the Faith.

"The Christian Brothers have been very good to us. We are coming from Long Beach to St. Mary's College. They are giving us refuge at this beautiful place, Moraga, where we may work in the kitchens and dining rooms and help make life homelike for the boys who attend the college.

"That is God's work too. Better that we do this now, serve God among his young, do you not think?"

Oakland

∞

On May 18, Mother Luisita and some other Sisters traveled to Oakland. The Brothers drove them right away to Providence Hospital, where they stayed with the other two Carmelites for three months while waiting for the completion of the construction of the new campus.

The Brothers' generosity seemed to know no limits. They hired an English teacher, Miss Valim, to tutor the Carmelites during their three-month stay in Oakland, and they pitched in to try to teach the Sisters some basic phrases and introduce them slowly to the culture. The Sisters' favorite moments with the Brothers were the quiet evenings when the Brothers joined them during their recreation hour and told stories about the history of Saint Mary's.

"Sisters, while you are here, could you kindly help us with our chapel and sacristy, especially with sewing?" Brother Gregory asked.

All of the Sisters were skilled in sewing, and they kept busy making curtains, vestments, and altar linens for the Brothers' chapel and sacristy. Keeping their hands busy with this sewing was a therapy of sorts for these women who had been through so much; it centered and calmed them. It was relaxing and proved to be just what they needed. Little by little, each one was recovering.

They scheduled time to do the English homework that Miss Valim assigned them. English was very difficult for many of them to learn, but they did understand more and more as the weeks went by.

About a month after his first interview, Fred Williams was ready to write the second of his three *Monitor* articles about these "exiled nuns of the Little Flower from Mexico," as he called them. He brought his daughter, Margaret Mary. He also brought a camera.

"Mother, may I take a picture of you with my daughter?" Was it the compassionate empathy he had shown these exiled Sisters of the Little Flower that touched Mother Luisita so much? Whatever it was, Mother Luisita said yes.

She held her large crucifix in one hand and quite spontaneously put her other arm around Margaret Mary, who looked up, smiled, and snuggled against Mother Luisita. Fred Williams seized the moment and quickly captured the endearing photo.

"Mother, may I take a picture of you and the Sisters around you? Please?" Again, Mother said yes, and as she sat down, the Sisters gathered around her, some standing, and some kneeling. Fred Williams took another intriguing photo.

The day the article and the photos were published, Williams brought Mother Luisita a copy of the paper. She asked Sister Margarita María to translate it for them during their evening recreation.

VIGNETTES FROM CATHOLIC LIFE
by Fred W. Williams
June 3, 1928

A ray of sunshine, filtering through a crack in the curtain, penetrates the cool shadows of the improvised chapel of the Carmelites at old Saint Mary's College in Oakland and forms a halo above the figure of the Christ on the Crucifix above the altar.

On its way to the Cross, it lingers caressingly on a solitary figure in the brown habit of Carmel that kneels many hours in prayer.

This is María Luisa, the Mother General of the exiled nuns of the Little Flower from Mexico.

The Sisters at the door to the chapel tell you the Mother General is not well, that she has not been well for a long time, ever since, in fact, the Holy Mother Church went under the iron heel of bitter persecution in Mexico.

Letters reach her every day. They are in Spanish, and they come from the faithful in the homeland. They tell of many things that sadden her heart, of the murder and torture of friends, of the striking down of good priests, so many of them, of the robbing of the Church and the scattering of her flocks.

Downstairs, a little group of nuns place flowers at the feet of a statue of Saint John Baptiste de la Salle, he who founded the Christian Brothers in the seventeenth century, who carried the light of education into the cellars and tenements of the poor.

They are so grateful to the Christian Brothers, these good nuns, for the Christian Brothers have been so good to them. When all of the world, it seemed, had turned against them, when they were upon the streets and without homes, the Christian Brothers did a splendid, gracious thing. They offered a haven from the conflict; they are building them a convent with a cloistered garden at Moraga, site of the new St. Mary's.

And so, each day they place fresh flowers at the feet of the statue of St. John Baptiste de la Salle, whose sons came to their aid in the answer to their prayers.

They pray for their Church now in Mexico, these little nuns, and for their Catholic countrymen and for their beloved Mother General, whose heart is so heavy and who, hour upon hour, like a statue carved in stone, kneels before the Blessed Sacrament.

IN THE FACE OF DARKNESS

María Luisa comes slowly down the stairs. She has finished with her prayers. Her nuns put forth willing hands to help her. Though not old, she has become feeble.

A gracious lady. A Spanish aristocrat. A woman who must have been a great beauty in her youth. Her eyes are big and brown and alight with strange fires. Now and then a troubled shadow quenches them. When she smiles, which is seldom, her whole face brightens, and the vista of years are swept away. Her eyes look on and past you. You sense she sees something you do not. Those eyes, so wondrous in their penetration, have looked upon tragedy and yet much happiness. Reverently you touch the hand she extends.

The Mother General does not speak English, but through a nun who acts as interpreter, she tells you something of her sorrows and of her unhappy land in which the Church lies so sorely wounded.

Her heart bleeds for the priests in Mexico, the priests who remained behind, who are cut down in their acts of mercy by the ruthless gunmen of "The Butcher" and who die with prayers of forgiveness for their murderers.

A bell tinkles softly against the coming night and summons the exiles of the Little Flower to Benediction. They gather their habits closely about them and silently, by twos, leave for the chapel.

Later in the evening, when all is silent about the deserted college building, golden voices rise from the Chapel singing the Latin hymn "Laudate Dominum."

At the end of July, Mother Luisita and Sister Margarita María went back to Long Beach with the intention of remaining there to welcome the new arrivals when they came in August and to help them in any way they could. They also wanted to accompany them on the train to San Francisco.

Back in Long Beach, Mother Luisita renewed her many friendships there. Not long after her return, she invited Father Joseph A. Vaughan, S.J., to celebrate Mass for the Sisters in the Chestnut Avenue house on July 31, the feast of Saint Ignatius of Loyola, founder of Father Vaughan's order, the Society of Jesus, also known as the Jesuits. Archbishop Francisco Orozco y Jiménez had counseled her to seek spiritual direction from the Jesuits whenever possible, so their yearly eight-day retreats would consist of the Spiritual Exercises of Saint Ignatius.

"Do we have a picture of Saint Ignatius that we can put in our chapel for his feast day?" Mother asked Sister Margarita María.

"I'll look, Mother."

There was none to be found. She went around the neighborhood, asking the neighbors if they knew of a store in Long Beach that sold Catholic articles. The answer was no, and they were told it would be necessary to go to Los Angeles. It was too late in the afternoon to travel, so a picture of Saint Ignatius would not grace their chapel on his feast day. Maybe next year.

That afternoon, Sister Margarita María, who was assigned to meet and greet visitors, went to answer the doorbell. An elderly peddler was standing there. He had such a strange accent that she was barely able to understand him. He began to bring out religious pictures to show her. It finally dawned on her that he was selling them.

About to turn him away, she suddenly remembered Mother Luisita's wish for a picture of Saint Ignatius—one large enough for the chapel—so she inquired, "Do you happen to have a picture of Saint Ignatius?"

"No, no," he replied, "the Blessed Mother, the Christ Child," but even as he was answering her question, he began searching through his pictures. Sister Margarita María prayed that he might have one. At the same time, the old man was muttering to himself that no one had ever asked for a picture of Saint Ignatius. At last, he pulled something out of the bottom of the pile, and a smile lit up his face. He held up a picture of Saint Ignatius, bowed low, and handed it to Sister Margarita María. It was not only a very good picture but was large enough for their chapel.

Suddenly Sister Margarita María remembered how poor they were. Such a picture must be very expensive, but she asked anyway. "How much is this picture?"

"Ten cents," the man replied.

In absolute disbelief, she repeated, "Ten cents?"

The old man just smiled. Sister Margarita María left him standing on the doorstep while she went flying up the stairs to Mother Luisita's room to show it to her and to tell her the price. The old man was still standing, waiting, when she returned and handed him the ten cents. He had packed away all his wares. He thanked her and went on his way.

Mother Luisita told her that evening, "Saint Ignatius has never failed to answer my prayers."

After Mass the next morning, Father Vaughan stayed for breakfast. He remarked, "I'm happy to see the picture of Saint Ignatius in your little chapel, Mother, and to know of your community's devotion to him." Referring to the picture, he added, "You must have brought that from Mexico. It is an unusually good picture."[21]

---

[21] This picture can be found in the archives of the motherhouse of the Carmelite Sisters of the Most Sacred Heart of Los Angeles in Alhambra, California.

Mother Luisita told him how they had just acquired it the day before and that the neighbors had told Sister Margarita María that no one else in the neighborhood had been visited by the peddler. She had mentioned it that same afternoon to the ladies in her catechism and sewing circle, and none of them had even seen the peddler, though they lived on the same block.

Only the Carmelites had seen him.

Chapter 23

Saint Mary's

There should always be something that we need so that we can ask Our Lord to supply it. May He be blessed!

—Letter to Sister Margarita María, 1934

The fourth group of exhausted Sisters arrived right on schedule during the sultry August days of 1928. Like the ones who came before them, they were unable to speak of their beloved homeland. Some seemed to be in shock, and all of them were malnourished. Mother Luisita and Sister Margarita María accompanied them on their four-hundred-mile train ride to San Francisco and their seven-mile boat trip to Oakland. Gratefully they discovered, as had the other Sisters before them, that the Bay Area was much cooler.

Now, the cohort of Sisters was complete. Eighteen Sisters would remain to fulfill the two-year contract with the Christian Brothers, while Mother Luisita and Sister Margarita María would stay only for a while and then return to Long Beach.

They all waited in Oakland until the construction of the new college and convent was completed. The day for their move from Oakland to Moraga finally arrived. The summer sun beat down on bus after bus loaded with things for the college and the newly built convent on the sixteen-mile trip from Oakland to Moraga. On the last trip, Mother Luisita and her eighteen Sisters boarded the bus. The last passenger to board was their chaplain, Father Diego Santos, a Franciscan priest who carried the Blessed Sacrament with him to the newly built Moraga chapel.

The Carmelite passengers led the Rosary and sang hymns during the trip, and, in deference to the Blessed Sacrament traveling with them, they maintained reverential silence. Only once, one of the Sisters leaned over and whispered to the Sister next to her, "Look at Mother Luisita. Look at her face. It is so radiant and recollected in the presence of the Blessed Sacrament on this bus."

It was true. Mother's face had assumed its radiance once again. Not realizing anyone was looking at her, she remained steeped in prayer until the driver stopped and turned off the motor in Moraga.

They were escorted to their new chapel so the Blessed Sacrament could be reserved in the tabernacle by Father Santos. The following Sunday, August 18, Archbishop Hanna blessed the new chapel, the convent, and the other buildings. Twelve new buildings dotted the beautiful campus. Students began arriving, and the fall semester began.

The Brothers noticed right away that something was wrong. The Sisters were experiencing too many hardships as they valiantly tried to fulfill their assigned tasks at Saint Mary's College. Five hundred students ate in the large student dining hall with its fourteen place settings per table, fourteen folded linen napkins, and a linen tablecloth on each of the thirty-five tables. Expensive chandeliers hung from the ceiling. The Carmelites were also responsible for the six other dining rooms, used by the Christian Brothers, the faculty, the staff, guests, and visitors. In addition, the Sisters took care of the sacristy and the laundering and folding of the gym clothes of the five hundred students.

They worked extremely hard — to the point of exhaustion. Many had come straight from Mexico, where they had been malnourished and deprived of health care during their months of hiding. Right away they got the flu. Mother Luisita noticed their weakness, but what could she do? Everything was new to them. It took them much longer to get things done than they or the Brothers had expected. There was always a Sister or two who was either sick or in tears from sheer exhaustion.

"Put down the dishes more carefully," Mother Luisita cautioned Sister Elena when she saw how she was placing a plate on a table while the previous one was still bouncing.

Sister Elena answered, "Mother, if even working so fast, we don't finish our work until eleven at night, what would it be like if I were to go slower?" It was true. They were keeping very late hours trying to catch up with all the work.

The Brothers, in their unparalleled charity, relieved the Sisters of the duties of washing the dishes and the boys' gym clothes, but the Sisters retained the duties of bussing the dishes after each meal, cleaning the tables, resetting all the places in all seven dining rooms, and mopping the floors. They also retained their sacristy and chapel duties. It was still too much for them.

They got sick, missed some of their required prayers, cut their sleeping hours, and eliminated recreation times. This schedule continued through October. One by one, the Sisters confided to Mother Luisita. "Mother Luisita, I'm embarrassed to tell you that I look forward to illness because it means a day off and some extra sleep."

"Mother, may I have my habit washed tomorrow? That way I can take a nap while it's being laundered and get some more sleep. I'm very tired."

"Mother, I'm coming down with still another cold. I'm sorry to ask again to go to bed earlier."

And on and on.

What shall I tell them, my Lord? How can I help them?

In December, most of the students left Saint Mary's to spend Christmas vacation at home with their families. The Sisters stayed at the college during the week of Christmas vacation. They had some extra time and could slow down and observe the Carmelite Christmas customs with more recollection and devotion.

Something profound was happening within Mother Luisita and the other Sisters. Their sojourn in Moraga brought about a spiritual purification within all of them. Suffering purifies. The words of the prophet Zechariah became the lived experience of Mother Luisita and her Sisters:

> I will ... refine them as one refines silver,
>   and test them as gold is tested.
> They will call on my name,
>   and I will answer them.
> I will say, "They are my people";
>   and they will say, "The LORD is my God." (13:9)

Moraga was the refiners' fire that removed the dross of imperfection and purified their souls.

These continuing trials were a part of that dark night that cleanses and purifies. Every vestige of pride or vanity was being whittled away, leaving their souls open and awaiting the inspirations of God. Reaching a new level in her love for God, Mother Luisita experienced a spiritual maturity.

Saint Mary's

Under the inspiration of the Holy Spirit on Christmas Eve, in the stillness of the night before Midnight Mass and with quiet determination, Mother Luisita tiptoed quietly to the chapel. She wanted to be alone for a while. Kneeling before the tabernacle, she gently removed a folded paper from her pocket. Unfolding it slowly and quietly, she placed it in her left hand and then made the Sign of the Cross. Reading from the paper, she began to pray softly and fervently her Christmas offering:

> Lord, do me the charity of accepting me as Your own; I do not have any of the virtues required for You to accept me, but look at Your own merits and my desires. Here I am, Lord. I offer myself to You without any reservations or conditions. I want to deny You nothing. Deign to accept me so that once and for all, I am in right relationship with You. I am here. I am Yours. Do with me as You will. Give me Your love, and make me suffer whatever You like and in whatever manner You want. I do not want to be anything. I want to be the target of Your justice where Your chastising arm would rest.
>
> If You are pleased with my life, here it is, Lord, any way You want it. Without breaking the fulfillment of my vows, I offer myself and all my life to You for sinners in atonement for the sins that are committed every day and for priests.
>
> My Jesus, give me the necessary strength to suffer whatever You want to give me—or rather, cut off, burn, destroy, annihilate whatever You want. Even though my desire is that my life will be consumed soon—and how I wish I could hasten its coming—yet I resign myself to Your Holy Will.

IN THE FACE OF DARKNESS

My Lord, I promise to accept gladly any interior sorrow, sickness, contempt, calumny, false testimony, and my life, whatever way You are pleased to have me.

And if my sufferings have any merit, I offer them for priests and in a very special way for my Sisters.

December 24, 1928, Moraga, California

Quietly Mother Luisita refolded the paper, placed it back in her pocket, and retraced her steps to her place in the chapel. She had proclaimed her fiat again on a new and deeper spiritual level.

On Christmas Day, the Sisters had time to relax together and tell stories about their first Christmas in Long Beach. It was fun to recall their early days at Holy Innocents and the many humorous mistakes they made as they tried to adapt to the language and culture.

"I wonder if the B.P.O.E. came by the house this morning again," Sister Carmen recalled.

"I can't wait to hear about how Las Posadas went this year," added Sister Josephine. Yes, they were interested in this family sharing of the many new experiences they had gone through together.

One of the Sisters who had arrived only in August asked, "Mother, I can't stop thinking about all the Sisters in Mexico. Do you think they have enough food?"

Everyone looked up and stopped what they were doing. All eyes were on Mother Luisita. The question had struck a chord that resounded throughout the group. It had touched a concern that remained like background music in their daily lives.

What are the Sisters in Mexico doing right now?

Mother answered, "I don't know. I wish I did."

It was here in Moraga that she had come to a deeper level of abandonment to God and a more intimate union with Him through prayer.

Father Pedro wrote a letter to Mother Luisita at least once every month, and Father Huerta wrote frequently also. Father Callahan and Father Ott faithfully kept in touch. Both visited the Sisters during their time in Moraga.

The signed contract was for two years' employment at Saint Mary's College, and they were bound and determined to fulfill it.

While Archbishop Orozco y Jiménez was visiting with them during his mandated exile from Mexico, the bell rang, calling the Sisters back to the dining rooms. He carefully observed their tired gait and grim determination as, one by one, they excused themselves and walked past him and back to the kitchen. He looked at Mother quizzically, as if to say, "What's going on here?"

Mother told him candidly about her exhausted Sisters and offered to show him around their work areas. As he went from place to place, he shook his head, turned to her, and said, "Mother, this kind of work was certainly not meant for your community."

Later, during the Holy Hour, he noticed that the Sisters were falling asleep in the chapel. When he mentioned it later that afternoon, Mother Luisita told him the following story.

"Your Excellency, many times, when the community is in adoration before Our Lord during their meditation, they are fast asleep. I hesitate, trying to decide whether to wake them up out of respect for the Lord, or let them sleep because they are so tired." She stopped for a moment to catch her breath.

"Go on, Mother."

"One day, our chaplain, Father Santos, came into the chapel during our Holy Hour, and he, too, saw their fatigue and said,

'God is the first to understand. He knows these dear Sisters are exhausted. Look at them. They are fast asleep.' I told him of my dilemma, and he told me to let them sleep because the next meal's work would begin soon."

Before Archbishop Orozco y Jiménez left, he turned to Mother Luisita and said, "Mother, as soon as possible, find a way to stop this domestic work and return to the apostolates for which your community was founded."

"Yes, Your Excellency, I will," she replied.

Please, my Lord, please show me how.

Chapter 24

Saint Patrick's

It isn't possible to do everything we would like to do.

—Letter to Mother Elena, 1934

On June 21, 1929, Mother Luisita, who had returned to Long Beach, learned that a peace accord had been signed by the Mexican government and the Catholic Church. It was both her birthday and her feast day. What a gift! While the Sisters in Moraga were receiving the news in Brother Gregory's office, Mother Luisita was in the Long Beach chapel, absorbed in prayer.

Thank You, my Lord, thank You. But, my Lord, what will we find? After the carnage, what will be left?

I need You just as much now as before, my Lord. Stay with me, my Lord, stay with me. Show me what You want me to do now.

The following day, June 22, 1929, Mother Luisita knew what she had to do first. She began a letter to the Christian Brothers, advising them that, because the country was now at peace, all of the Carmelite Sisters would be leaving Saint Mary's in one year—in June 1930—when their contract terminated.

At the same time, Father Pedro had written Mother Luisita a letter informing her that the superior general of the Discalced Carmelites, Father William of Saint Albert, had left Rome and

181

would be visiting the various Carmelite communities in the United States. Since the very beginning of Mother Luisita's new community, Father Pedro had been their main contact with the Carmelite Order. As vice provincial and visitator of the Mexican Province, he was designated to oversee and visit the Mexican Carmelite communities. Finally, Mother Luisita would connect with the Carmelite father general, and he would learn firsthand about the curved path of the founding of this new, fervent Carmelite community.

The Very Reverend Father William of Saint Albert, superior general, arrived in the United States in June 1929 and began traveling to the various Carmels there. His visit to the Sisters at Saint Mary's was scheduled for August.

It was this visit of the superior general of all the Discalced Carmelites throughout the world that became the highlight of the Sisters' two years in Moraga. Father Pedro had taught them the correct protocol for receiving the Carmelite superior general, and they had learned well and followed Father Pedro's instructions exactly.

Since Mother Luisita had already returned to Long Beach, Mother Mary of the Eucharist, now the local superior of the Moraga community, welcomed the superior general and escorted him to the chapel. All the Sisters wore their white mantles and sang the Te Deum. Mother Mary then led the superior general to the community room of their convent, where he spoke to all the Sisters. He was very cordial and listened carefully when they shared with him their experiences during the persecution. He heard about how they had made their vows while in hiding, and about their struggles and other experiences while making their retreat in a corral next to the horses, and about their escape from the soldiers over the rooftops. They spoke about their near starvation at times. He listened carefully and gave them the gift of his wholehearted encouragement and approval.

Toward the end of his visit, he congratulated them for having persevered amid so many struggles. He spoke to them with affection and gave them gifts. Before he left, he mentioned that he would also visit Mother Luisita in Long Beach later that month, and then he gave them all his blessing.

In August 1929, something else occurred. Father Ott learned that he was being transferred from Holy Innocents in Long Beach to Saint Patrick's Church in Los Angeles. The move took place quickly, and within a few days, Father Ott's personal belongings were at Saint Patrick's, and a new pastor was on his way to Holy Innocents. The Sisters waited for Father Ott on the front porch of the house he had purchased for them. He got out of his car, walked up to the porch, and looked at them. Not much was said. How could they speak with the tight lumps in their throats and the tears ready to flow? He had become their dear and trusted friend and adviser.

Father Ott said gently, "Let's keep in touch, Sisters. You know where to find me in Los Angeles if you need me."

The new pastor at Holy Innocents took up his duties. He drove to the Chestnut Avenue house and knocked on the door. Sister Margarita María answered. "Good morning, Father. Won't you please come in?"

"Thank you, Sister. It won't take too long. May I make an appointment to see Mother, or would it be possible to speak with her for a few minutes now?"

"Surely, Father. Please sit down, and I'll see if she can see you now. I'll be right back."

She went upstairs and knocked on Mother Luisita's door. Mother opened it right away.

"Mother, our new pastor is downstairs. He wants to speak with you," she whispered.

"Of course, I'll go now," answered Mother Luisita.

The priest stood up as she entered the room and extended her hand to him. "Good morning, Father. Thank you for coming."

She glanced over to Sister Margarita María, who continued, "I usually interpret for Mother, as I know more English at this time."

"Of course, Sister. Please be seated. First of all, I want you to know that I've seen all of the good work you have done here in the parish in setting up catechetical centers for our Mexican immigrants."

He looked at Sister Margarita María and said, "Sister, I'll pause after every phrase to give you time to translate. It is very important that this conversation be heard and understood. Is that agreeable to you?"

"Certainly, Father, I'm happy to translate for you."

"Please inform Mother that your religious instruction in Spanish for the Mexican people will no longer be needed here at Holy Innocents. The work that you Sisters are doing is really quite unnecessary at this time. The financial burden created by your work can no longer be assumed by the parish, and only your rent and utilities will be paid by the parish from now on.

"Do you have any questions I may answer at this time?" he added.

Sister Margarita María translated. In her gracious manner, Mother Luisita remained steady as she summarized in Spanish what she understood, and Sister Margarita María conveyed the summary back to the pastor, who nodded and said, "Yes, that is correct."

He stood up to leave and then spoke once again to Sister Margarita María. "Sisters, please do not hesitate to come by and see me if you have any comments or think of any questions regarding what I said today."

"Yes, Father, we understand." Sister Margarita María couldn't say anything more because the knot in her chest was becoming tighter. Her heart was pounding so hard that it seemed as if it would break through her chest. She held back her tears so he wouldn't see her cry. Glancing at Mother Luisita, she saw her same, sweet face but noticed that her hands were clasped tightly with whitened knuckles as she continued to hold in her own tears. Both Mother Luisita and Sister Margarita María had determined that this new pastor would absolutely not see them cry.

And he didn't.

As soon as he left, the two women looked at each other and walked to the chapel, where they sat together in silence. Neither one had words to express her feelings. Although they seemed to be without a visible reaction, the reality was that they were totally stunned.

Later that day, Mother Luisita phoned Father Ott. His own presentiment was confirmed the moment she began relating what had happened. Without a moment's hesitation, he replied, "Mother, will you bring the Sisters to Saint Patrick's? My parishioners have such great need for you. There are many who speak little or no English. They would welcome you with open arms. If you will come, I will contact the chancery office and take care of everything. We'll find another house for you. I'm getting quite good at finding them, you know." Father Ott was a man of deep faith with a heart of gold.

Coming from an immigrant family, he understood the Sisters' predicament. He didn't have a house to offer them or work that they could do. Yet he wanted them to know, without a doubt, that they were welcome not only at Saint Patrick's, but more importantly, in the United States.

He had already noticed that there was an empty lot across the street from Saint Patrick's. His best option was to move a vacant house onto the lot. He had done it before, and he could do it again.

Right away he began calling on priests and friends, as well as a few realtors, to see if any of them knew of a vacant house that could be moved onto the lot across the street from Saint Patrick's. One of the neighboring pastors, Monsignor Joseph J. Truxaw, heard that Father Ott was looking for a place for the Carmelite Sisters to live and offered him the vacant convent in his parish. The only condition was that either he or the Sisters would have to assume the cost of moving it.

Father Ott told all this to Mother Luisita, including the sad fact that because Saint Patrick's had no funds to move the convent, the Sisters would have to assume the cost of moving it.

Mother replied, "I'll take care of it."

And she did.

She turned to Sister Margarita María and said, "Will you please call the chancery office and ask if I may have an emergency appointment with Father Callahan and the bishop?"

She got her appointment, and it didn't take long to explain the situation. The bishop already knew that, until recently, the vacant convent had been the residence of the Sisters of Saint Joseph of Carondelet. He readily agreed to cosign a bank loan for $3,500 to move the convent to Saint Patrick's.[22]

---

[22] The Archdiocese of Los Angeles cosigned a bank loan with Mother Luisita in 1929 so an abandoned convent could be

"Well, will you just look at that!" Father Ott was amazed and more than a little amused that his lessons on how to get things done in the United States had been so well understood by the Sisters.

The house was moved immediately to 1045 East Forty-Fifth Street, directly across from Saint Patrick's Church. On August 29, 1929, the Sisters arrived to occupy their new convent, which they placed immediately under the patronage of Saint Thérèse of Lisieux.

Father Ott shared some good news with them: "Sisters, I want you to know that this house will be the first property that you will own in the United States. The paperwork of this property shows that the Carmelite Sisters own it."

The call finally came telling the Sisters that Father William of Saint Albert would like to meet them. They were still living in Long Beach, so it was there that he met the foundress of this new Carmelite community.

---

moved onto the empty lot in front of Saint Patrick's Church. Although it did not take place until six years after Mother Luisita's death, the way in which the $3,500 note was finally paid belongs to the story of her first foundation in Los Angeles.

The Salesians of Saint John Bosco took over Saint Patrick's Parish in October 1943. The lot had grown in value, carrying the building with it as an integral part of the realty. The Sisters had not a scrap of paper in evidence of their equity in the property, but their moral claim was recognized, and the Salesians paid them $3,800 for the house. After discharging the note, they still had $300 left, which helped them establish the Little Flower Missionary House on its present site of 2434 Gates Street in Los Angeles. William M. Queen, *The Doctor's Widow* (Fresno, CA: Academy Library Guild, 1956), 95–96.

IN THE FACE OF DARKNESS

The visit went very well. The approval and blessing of the superior general of the order confirmed that Mother Luisita was following the path of God's holy will. She felt refreshed and spiritually renewed.

Adelante! Onward!

After moving into their new home in Los Angeles, the Sisters set up several Christian doctrine centers so the children would not have to travel too far from their homes to receive instruction in the Faith. By the time school opened in September, they were already teaching catechism in these centers. The parishioners grew to love the Sisters very much.

At the time of their move to Saint Patrick's, the Sisters brought with them a net profit of fifty dollars from their secondhand Long Beach store. It wasn't much, but it was something.

It was time for the Sisters' yearly eight-day retreat. Father Caballero, S.J., of Loyola High School was their retreat master. Mother offered him their fifty dollars as a stipend, but he refused to accept it, so they used the money for a pair of glasses for Sister Josephine and a pair of shoes for another Sister who needed them.

The extreme poverty they had experienced in Long Beach didn't lessen when they moved to Los Angeles. Father Ott was attentive to their needs as always, but Mother was reluctant to burden him, so he had no idea that they were barely subsisting. They did a little embroidery work to support themselves. When Father Ott gave them ten dollars and told them to sew new veils, the Sisters promptly applied the money to the milk bill. The Sisters still had only one habit each.

Summer merged into fall, and soon winter's rainy season arrived in full force. Several storms succeeded each other, with a new one coming in just as the previous storm was rolling out. For almost a week, there had been one steady downpour after another. The ground was saturated, and many streets were flooded. The gutters were filled with rushing water.

All that week the Sisters had subsisted on potatoes, the only food they had, and there was no money to buy anything else. When the rain stopped, two of the Sisters asked Mother Luisita, "Mother, may we have twenty-five cents? One of the parishioners told us that the butcher gives her all the bones she wants for her dog for only twenty-five cents." As an afterthought, she continued, "And they are good, clean bones. We thought that the butcher would give us twenty-five cents' worth of those bones, and we could make soup."

Mother Luisita knew how hungry they were. She was just as famished, and so she gave them the twenty-five cents, reminding them as they left to pray as they walked along the streets.

It hurt her that they were so poor that they needed to ask for bones. It was embarrassing and humiliating. She was mortified.

The Sisters prayed to Saint Joseph as they walked to the butcher shop. Suddenly Sister Margarita María heard, "Look! Look down! Isn't that a roll of money in the gutter?" She stepped down and picked up from the gutter the dirty, soggy wad. It was money all right, thoroughly soaked.

Instead of continuing to the butcher shop, they returned to show Mother Luisita what they had found. They were so excited that they hadn't even attempted to unroll the wad of bills. Mother Luisita began to count: twenty, forty, sixty, seventy dollars. The Sisters were as excited as children over their discovery, but Mother Luisita was more serious. She said, "It is not ours, you know. We must try to find the owner. We cannot keep this money."

The other Sisters looked at each other. Sister Margarita Maria broke the silence. "Mother, I think that it would be practically impossible to find the owner. It looks as if these bills were washed along the gutter for perhaps a long way."

Mother was adamant. "Try to find the owner."

Sister Margarita María had an idea. "Mother, may we call Father Ott and ask him what he thinks is best for us to do?"

"Yes, I trust Father Ott. Go ahead and ask him."

After listening to the account of how and where the money was found, Father Ott assured the Sisters that it would be quite impossible to find the owner. He said, "Tell Mother Luisita that the good Lord must have intended the money for you, so go ahead and use it."

They told Mother his answer. She asked, "Sisters, you didn't tell him you were on your way to buy dog bones, did you?"

"Of course not. We just told him we found the money in the gutter." It never again became necessary for them to try to buy bones put aside for the dogs.

The newly moved convent had more space than the Sisters needed. After they had lived in the house for several months, the director of the Catholic Welfare Bureau called to ask whether the Carmelite Sisters would take in some boarding girls who had no place to go. He said that it would be a temporary placement.

"Yes," Mother Luisita answered right away. "Please tell him yes."

Nine girls arrived. The large convent was the first happy home most of them had ever known. The Sisters packed lunches for the older girls who attended nearby schools, helped with their homework, put their hair in curlers, and applied first aid to cuts and bruises. They were the arbitrators in their little quarrels, and the Sisters' words were accepted as final.

The Sisters not only accepted young girls as boarding students; they also provided many programs for Mexican refugees — offering homemaking skills and parenting classes to the people of the neighborhood and an Association of Christian Mothers. Mother Luisita established the Juventud Catolica Femenina Mexicana (Mexican Women's Catholic Youth Group) and asked Sister Teresita of the Child Jesus to take charge of the group. In addition, the Sisters visited homes and took the Saint Patrick's parish census.

"Has anyone seen Mother Luisita?" asked Sister Teresita. "We're getting a new girl today. I just received a phone call from Catholic Welfare."

"You should know where she is," whispered Sister Refugio, who leaned her head toward the chapel.

Sister Teresita tiptoed down the hallway and peeked into the chapel. Sure enough, there was Mother Luisita, kneeling in prayer, head bent in adoration. Mother Luisita was having another heart-to-heart conversation with God.

In just a few more months, the Sisters will leave Saint Mary's. Lord, please let me know if You want us all to go back to Mexico or if You want us to continue what we have begun here in the United States when we finish our contract at Saint Mary's.

And, my God, one more thing: Is what I heard true? Is it true that even though the peace accord was signed, thousands of Cristeros are still being killed out of retaliation?

I thought it was all over.

Chapter 25

The Next Steps

*The prayer of one soul alone united to that of
Jesus in the tabernacle can save the world.*

—From the spiritual notes of Mother Luisita

Four months after the signing of the peace accord, Mother Luisita returned to Mexico. However, in the Los Altos region of Jalisco, where the Cristero uprising had begun, the war was not over. Former Cristeros were still being targeted by local guerillas who had fought alongside the federal soldiers and now were taking their own revenge in the small towns, despite the signing of the peace accord. In some places, the Cristeros were massacred even as they were laying down their arms at a local church.[23]

---

[23] "To their credit more than one Federal general warned the former Cristeros of the upcoming revenge of the local inhabitants. One general, Andrès Figueroa, warned the Cristeros, 'Go *very far away. . . . They will kill you all soon. It will do you no good to go around armed. I am here as a representative of the Federal Government and I give you my word as a gentleman that you have no reason to fear me. But these little local politicians always think they are doing Mexico a favor by committing outrages like these. . . . They will also satisfy their thirst for vengeance.'*

IN THE FACE OF DARKNESS

Mother Luisita learned that when Pope Pius XI had authorized Archbishop Leopoldo Ruiz y Flóres to sign the peace accord, he imposed two conditions: (1) that amnesty would be granted to all those in arms who surrendered and (2) that houses, bishops' residences, and seminaries would be returned. The president immediately accepted both conditions.

These conditions, however, were never fulfilled. As a consequence, Mother Luisita returned to a country that was not at peace and where vengeance continued, especially in Los Altos, where both her community and the Cristiada were born. Evidence of the carnage was apparent throughout Los Altos. The land, the ranches, the cattle and agricultural fields, and the financial holdings of many of her friends and acquaintances were gone. Remnants of the violent battles covered the land. It seemed as if she could hear the anguished cries rising from the very soul of her beloved Mexico.

Amidst the ruins and the rubble, she had an idea that she wanted to carry out: 1929 was the twenty-fifth anniversary of the beginnings of the Carmelite community, and she wanted to have a party. It was simple and subdued, but the Sisters pulled it off, and it exceeded their expectations, a grand fiesta, albeit a hidden and quiet one.

With Archbishop Orozco y Jimenez's permission, the constitutions and ceremonial books were approved right away, and

---

"His words proved accurate. Immediately after the Peace Accord was signed, a more direct and personal persecution began—the systematic, premeditated assassination of the Cristero leaders for the purpose of preventing the renewal of the movement. By the time it was over the manhunt claimed 5,000 victims." Meyer, *The Cristiada*, 178–179.

his permission to reopen and then to transfer the novitiate to Guadalajara came two months later.

Mother Luisita had been in Mexico for only a few months trying her best to reorganize her hospital, schools, and convents when Archbishop Orozco y Jiménez, still living in exile in the United States, contacted her.

"Mother, I want to speak with you personally. Return to the United States immediately."

I have more to do, Lord. You know that I need more time here in Mexico, Lord. Of course, though, I will leave right away.

Mother, together with her traveling companion, Sister Margarita María, arrived in Los Angeles on January 21, 1930. At the door of Saint Patrick's convent, Mother sensed that something new had taken place.

Turning to Sister Margarita María, she asked, "Don't you sense something is different here? What is it? Do you feel it?"

They stood by the front door for several minutes and listened. Suddenly Mother Luisita realized what had changed and smiled.

My Sisters are laughing! Such lovely, natural laughter! It sounds so right!

In spending time with the Sisters, she discovered that they were learning to like, even love, both America and Americans. The Carmelites in the United States were adjusting to the new culture.

The wounds of war were healing.

Within the next few months, Mother Luisita had several meetings with Archbishop Orozco y Jiménez. He was the only Mexican bishop who did not agree to the peace accord with the government. He was steadfast in his belief that it did not go far enough because the articles of the constitution against religion were not removed or changed. He would not, he could not, go back to Mexico, so he stayed in the United States in exile until such time as the constitutional articles against the Church would be removed.[24]

"Mother," the archbishop told her, "I called you back because I have been thinking of your Carmelite community. I want your Sisters to remain in the United States and find a way to prepare a novitiate house here, close to the border. I'm afraid that your Sisters in Mexico will experience extreme danger in the near future, and I am most concerned about your novices."

Deep lines etched his weary face. His many exiles, both now and during the previous Mexican Revolution, and his years spent in jail under oppressive regimes had taken their toll. As the shepherd of his oppressed and scattered flock, he keenly felt his responsibility to help the Carmelite Sisters, even though he was so far from his archdiocese. "Have a house ready in the United States so that at a moment's notice we can bring the novices in Mexico up here, should that become necessary. There is a second wave of persecution still to come. I'm sure of it.

"When you return to Mexico, convoke a chapter meeting right away, and just go ahead and appoint a new governing body

---

[24] The peace accord was signed through the diplomatic efforts of Pope Pius XI, the Mexican bishops, the Mexican government, and the United States with Ambassador Dwight Morrow as the arbitrator. These diplomatic efforts had been going on simultaneously with the Cristero Revolt. See Most Reverend Francis Clement Kelley, *Blood-Drenched Altars: A Catholic Commentary on the History of Mexico* (Rockford, IL: Tan Publishers, 1995), 463–464.

for your community. Stay in close touch so that we can make the right decisions."

Mother Luisita agreed with everything the archbishop had said. "Yes, Your Excellency. I will. My preference, also, is to establish the congregation officially, canonically, both in Mexico and in the United States."

Before returning to Mexico, she met with Father Callahan, who told her, "Mother, I would like you to consider establishing a Catholic tuberculosis sanatorium in the Archdiocese of Los Angeles. Ever since 1927, when your Sisters arrived, I have kept in close contact with your community. I have followed with great interest all of your activities at Holy Innocents and Saint Patrick's. I have observed your Sisters' dedication to God and to the parish and to the civic community as well. I have seen your Sisters' unselfishness, their practice of poverty, their resourcefulness, and their cheerfulness. And, Mother, I understand your vision and mission of uniting the spirit of Carmel with the active apostolate."

He moved his chair a little closer to where Mother Luisita was sitting.

"I am aware, however, that unless your community sinks deeper roots, makes a more permanent commitment to the archdiocese, I cannot guarantee that you will be able to remain in the United States and survive. The government is beginning to enforce the new Repatriation Act, by which refugees and other immigrants from Mexico are taken back to their original homeland. You must be firmly settled here, Mother. Tuberculosis is rampant right now, as you know, and there is a real need for Spanish-speaking patients to be able to communicate with their caregivers. That is why I am telling you about my dream of establishing a sanatorium. I think your community is the right one to do this."

As usual, Mother Luisita was straightforward and respectful. "Father, it is not that I'm opposed to your idea. I'm simply wondering if it is a little premature. I don't know if we are ready for so big a step—to build and take over the operation of a sanatorium. I will pray over this and let you know my decision."

Mother Luisita met with the Sisters that afternoon and spoke about Father Callahan's plans. She ended with the following words: "Remember the $3,500 loan we took out from the bank last year so we could move the Saint Patrick's convent onto the empty lot? Only God knows when that will be paid off. This debt weighs very heavily on my heart. You all know how much I am the enemy of debt.

"And our Sisters at Saint Mary's will remain in Moraga only until the end of June. We need to find the right place for them to live after they leave Moraga, and I really don't know yet if they should remain here or go back to Mexico."

There was one piece that Mother Luisita had withheld from the Sisters. Father Callahan had told her that the community would need to finance the new tuberculosis sanatorium.

She remembered the October stock market crash, the worst economic depression in the history of the United States. Mother understood the impact of this crash on Father Callahan's request. She realized that this changed everything. All previous plans had to be rethought and adapted to the dire financial circumstances of the United States. The Diocese of Los Angeles had very little money now. The Carmelite Sisters would have to finance the sanatorium. That is what Father Callahan had said.

Lord, how can we possibly finance the construction of a tuberculosis sanatorium? The only solution that comes to mind is to use the money from my mother's inheritance to establish the sanatorium. There is no other way.

She traveled back to Mexico to follow through on the archbishop's directive to call a general meeting and replace the governing body of the congregation. This convocation would have been called in 1927 if the times had been normal, but the upheaval caused by the persecution had prevented it. Even now, it was not a matter of convening the customary election protocol, the ordinary general chapter, in which, based on elections and other canonical requisites, a new governing body could be formed. Instead, Mother Luisita herself was to name a general council and continue as superior in compliance with the orders of the archbishop, who did not allow her to resign as she had hoped. The next months were extremely busy ones, both in Mexico and in the United States. Things kept changing as Mother Luisita was trying to make her decisions. Still using her coded words, she continued writing letters. Her only communication between countries was through these letters.

She took up her pen again and began writing. "When Our Lord has taken a soul for His very own, He does with it whatever pleases Him most, and He disposes everything according to His sublime and just purposes. What happens is that we're shortsighted and can't understand it."

She was tired now and put the unanswered letters back into the bag.

Time was running out as Mother Luisita continued to weigh the various options for her community. As these matters were being worked out, she received a letter announcing that Father Ott was being transferred to San Diego.

Blessed be God!

Chapter 26

Santa Teresita

A word said in the name of God may bring
about the salvation of a soul.

—Letter to Sister Margarita María, 1929

It was one of those hot, muggy nights in Los Angeles. The air was so still that the only sound was the hum of the resident mosquitoes. Sister Margarita María couldn't sleep. The stuffy room combined with the noise from the ambulances arriving at the emergency hospital across the street boded another sleepless night. Just this afternoon, one of the Sisters had told her, "I think I will go crazy if I have to listen to those sirens all night long again in this oppressive heat."

Mother Luisita was also awake. She was trying to put together the puzzle pieces that would determine the future course of her community in the United States.

Should I give permission for the Sisters to open a sanatorium
for victims of tuberculosis in the United States?[25]

---

[25] In 1900, "the three leading causes of death were pneumonia, tuberculosis (TB), and diarrhea and enteritis, which (together with diphtheria) caused one third of all deaths." "Achievements

IN THE FACE OF DARKNESS

Can we learn the nursing protocols for this terrible disease?
Can we be assured that we will always have patients?
My Lord, is this Your will for us?

Mother mulled over Father Callahan's explanation of the need for a tuberculosis sanatorium for Spanish-speaking girls and young women who were victims of this white plague.[26]

She recalled his conclusion word for word. "I can tell you this, Mother. This is a need your Sisters can fill. I would like to go with Mother Mary and Sister Margarita María to see if the bishop would give permission for your community to do this work here in the archdiocese with the Spanish-speaking tuberculosis patients. Would you please consider this option of opening a tuberculosis sanatorium so the Carmelite Sisters can remain in the United States?"

After much prayer, she decided to go ahead with the opening of the tuberculosis sanatorium. Picking up her pen once again, she wrote to Mother Mary of the Eucharist and told her that she would be the local superior at the new sanatorium, and Sister Margarita María would be the administrator. She delegated her to give this news to Father Callahan in her name in an official letter.

Soon after receiving Mother Luisita's letter, Mother Mary and Sister Margarita María made their way to Father Callahan's

---

in Public Health, 1900-1999: Control of Infectious Diseases," *Morbidity and Mortality Weekly Report* 48, no. 29 (July 30, 1999), https://www.cdc.gov/mmwr/preview/mmwrhtml/mm4829a1. htm.

[26] "In the first decades of the 20th century, one out of every 170 Americans lived in a sanatorium." PBS, *The Forgotten Plague: Tuberculosis in America*, directed by Chana Gazit, aired February 10, 2015, transcript, https://www.pbs.org/wgbh/americanexperience/films/plague/.

office in the Higgins Building to tell him the news. He was elated and wanted to move forward immediately.

In June 1930, Mother Mary of the Eucharist, Sister Margarita María, and Father Callahan met with Bishop Cantwell, who listened attentively, but at first he was very reluctant to give his approval. He spoke candidly of the financial risk involved, of their lack of experience, and of the youth of Father Callahan and the Sisters who were present. Father Callahan, Mother Mary, and Sister Margarita María were under thirty years of age.

At last the bishop said, "All right. You have my approval, but you must start on a small scale."

After the three left the bishop's office, Father Callahan was already in gear to find the ideal location for the new sanatorium. Every day he searched the newspapers, spoke with realtors, or attended auctions, but he just couldn't find a suitable property. At last, one day he came to Saint Patrick's with good news.

"Sisters, I have great news for you! A three-acre tract with a small house is now available for purchase. It is in Duarte, California, only twenty-two miles east of Los Angeles. It lies in the San Gabriel Valley, a charming valley similar to the Atotonilco valley of your native state of Jalisco, surrounded by the foothills of the San Gabriel Mountains."

Mother Mary asked, "What is the asking price?"

"Seventeen thousand five hundred dollars."

A little gasp. "Oh, my!" was all she could get out.

The next day, they drove to Duarte to see the property. They immediately fell in love with the three-acre plot of land that reminded them so much of their home in Jalisco.

It needed a lot of work, but they were willing to roll up their sleeves and begin. With Mother Luisita's approval, the Sisters borrowed $17,500 from the bank for the property and another

$5,000 for equipment with a first and a second mortgage on the property. The diocese guaranteed the loans because the Sisters, without funds of their own, were assuming a large debt.

This was a huge leap of faith on the part of the bishop and on the part of Mother Luisita.

On July 8, 1930, nine Sisters were living in the Duarte farm-house. Mother Mary of the Eucharist was the local superior. Sister Soledad was the local vicar, a role similar to that of a vice president. Sister Margarita María was assigned as the administrator. They had only twenty-five days to get the property ready for the arrival of the first patients, who were scheduled to come on August 2, 1930, the feast of Our Lady of the Angels.

The next day, they placed an ad in the *Los Angeles Examiner* requesting furniture — anything usable — for the sanatorium. Many odds and ends came in, and every item was used. Stacked wooden packing crates became patients' nightstands. Sixteen totally unmatched chairs graced the dining tables for the patients. The only new items were dishes the Sisters bought at the five-and-dime store.

Father Callahan, with help from his family, converted the garage into a recreation hall for ambulatory patients, and the two shacks that were renamed "cottages" became wards for the patients.

One day, an old Cathedral High School bus rambled slowly onto the property. Cathedral High School in Los Angeles was staffed by the same Christian Brothers they knew in Moraga. When the door opened, Father Callahan stepped out, grinning. "Sisters, I've managed to get you this old bus from Cathedral High School. I think you can use the seats from it for the girls' recreation room."

Sure enough, the seats made comfortable chairs for the ambulatory patients.

It was fun to do the impossible—and incredibly hard work!

The Sisters rented a sewing machine for two days—for that was all they could afford—and used it around the clock. They took eight-hour sewing shifts and sewed patient gowns, curtains, rugs, towels, washcloths, bed linen, and whatever else could be made from cloth.

There was no hot running water anywhere on the property. "How will we sterilize everything, Sisters, if we have no hot water?" Mother Mary asked. "Tuberculosis is highly contagious."

By that evening, they had the answers they needed. Sister Margarita María summarized what they had learned. "Sisters, we need to find a clearing outside to chop firewood. We have many trees that are old and dying that can be used for firewood, and I'm sure we can find out where to get more wood, as we will need it. We will use very large pots, some for dishes and some for bed linen and clothing. It will be a lot of hard work, but we are young, and we can do it!"

"How long do you need to boil the dishes?" asked Sister María de las Victorias.

"Twenty minutes in boiling water with the recommended solution will completely sterilize them," answered Sister Margarita María.

And so, by coming together, using their common sense, and asking questions, some of which they could answer themselves and others they referred to friends who knew how to find the correct answers, the Sisters learned what they needed to do to open and operate the new sanatorium.

Because they could not afford to hire any staff, they became carpenters and painters as they found new uses for fruit crates.

Other Sisters worked at trimming and weeding; some helped clean up the property. They improvised tools and furnishings. Mother Mary spent every morning sweeping the property while battling the huge pockets of wild undergrowth throughout the three acres that were home to snakes and other reptiles.

Every minute of every day was filled to the brim with getting everything ready. On July 30, Father Callahan told them, "I'll be by tomorrow, Sisters, at 8:00 a.m. to celebrate the first Mass."

July 31 was the feast of Saint Ignatius. It was two years ago exactly since the mysterious peddler had come by their Long Beach house to sell his wares and offered to sell the "miracle" painting of Saint Ignatius for only ten cents. This year, Our Lord gave them another gift — the celebration of their first Mass there. There was no chapel, only a makeshift altar. There were no vestments. Father Callahan brought with him the essentials for Mass — the chalice, cruets, hosts, missal, crucifix, and some altar wine. When it came time for the Mass to begin, everyone realized that he had not brought vestments with him, and he had forgotten his cassock.

"Don't worry, Father; we'll improvise," offered Mother Mary. After a few minutes of quick thinking and looking around their sparse farmhouse, they quickly removed the sleeves of a new brown habit.

"Here, Father, please put this on. It will be your cassock and alb today," Mother Mary said as she helped him slip the brown, now-sleeveless tunic over his head.

Next, they spied ribbon on a gift package. The ribbon was long enough to fit around his waist as a cincture. Sister Margarita María whispered to Father Callahan as she gave him the ribbon, "Please disregard the fact that it is pink, Father."

He was beside himself with amusement. Thank God there was no mirror around. Better that he didn't know how he looked.

There was no missal stand, but packing-case filler stuffed in some material worked fine.

They knelt, and Mass began. Before long, tears flowed as they wept spontaneously in gratitude for their religious freedom, their friends, and their new (and first) benefactors. This first Mass, with Father Callahan wearing a partial Carmelite habit with the ribbon cincture, became one of those never-to-be-repeated moments of life.

There was one most important detail not yet confirmed—the name of the sanatorium. Ever faithful to his favorite Carmelite saint, Thérèse of Lisieux, Father Callahan asked that she be patroness of the new sanatorium.

He reminded the Sisters that Saint Thérèse herself had been a victim of tuberculosis and would, therefore, be an inspiration to the patients as they learned of her courage and holiness. Her youth, too, would appeal to them, for she was only twenty-four when she died.

What about my promise I made to You, my Lord, that all of our hospitals will be dedicated to Your Sacred Heart? Should I make an exception this one time out of deference to Father Callahan? It means so much to him, Lord.

Finally she made up her mind. "Yes," she wrote the Sisters, "go ahead—the name will be Santa Teresita Rest Home."

Chapter 27

Primorosas

When Our Lord sends you occasions to practice virtue
in any manner whatsoever, don't oppose Him or resist.
Accept with good will the difficulties and contradictions
of life. I would like very much for you to become a great
soul, strong and vigorous, never looking toward your
own gain and self-love, but toward God's glory.

—Letter to Sister Margarita María, 1935

Midmorning on August 2, 1930, the Sisters heard the ambulance
from Olive View Sanatorium laboring up the unpaved road to
Santa Teresita Rest Home. Five young girls were lifted out, frightened and crying. They were all very sick.

It didn't take long for the girls to notice that the Carmelite
Sisters genuinely cared about them, that their service to them
was authentic. These young patients, because of their lack of
English, had learned to become demanding in order to get their
needs met. Here they observed the kindness of the Sisters. They
noticed that the Sisters offered to do something for them even
before they asked. They anticipated their needs and gave them
attention and comfort.

IN THE FACE OF DARKNESS

Saint John of the Cross, the Carmelite mystic and Doctor of the Church, wrote, "Where there is no love, give love and you will draw forth love." This is what was happening at Santa Teresita. This was also the charism of Mother Luisita's new community—to bring God's healing love to body and soul.

This is how her community began.

This is how the community continued.

"Why are you doing this for us? We see how hard you work and how tired you are. And who is this Santa Teresita you mention so often?" The girls were amazed that there was no running hot water anywhere on the property. They watched in amazement as the Sisters chopped wood with heavy axes and built fires three times a day to boil water in enormous pots. Watching the Sisters laugh as they worked was great fun and gave the girls something interesting to do as the hours passed.

Father Harold E. Ring, S.J., rector of Loyola High School, agreed to drive thirty miles from Los Angeles every First Friday of the month to celebrate Mass at the little sanatorium.

An almost visible atmosphere of peace and cheerfulness began to permeate Santa Teresita. The number of girls increased from five to sixteen to twenty-eight to forty. The county continued to reimburse Santa Teresita for the same amount for each patient.

Time passed quickly. Daily life settled into a routine. The Carmelite Sisters were digging deeper roots in California's soil as they transplanted the principles and values of the Carmelite charism of Mother Luisita into the United States. Their day-to-day, wholehearted, disciplined beginnings became often repeated stories passed along at first through letters to their Sisters in Mexico and then to the families they served and the people of the local Duarte community.

Although the early days at Santa Teresita were very difficult, as the days passed, each cottage became a home to the six or eight girls living there. Visitors began to notice the family spirit. The girls began to share their stories about their lives before they came to Santa Teresita and the transformation in their hearts.

Mercedes Limón came to Santa Teresita less than three months after it opened. She was twelve years old and an orphan. There was no possibility, aside from a miracle, that she could ever recover. Both of her lungs were terminally infected. She was too weak to be up and around and was not permitted out of bed.

Mercedes was a very bright, cheerful child, naturally serious. Everyone liked her. She asked the Sisters many questions, especially about the little Carmelite, Santa Teresita, who also had suffered from tuberculosis and who was now a saint by doing just ordinary things with love. After she thought about that, a definite change began to take place in her. She now had a purpose, a goal in mind, and she was determined to do all she could to reach it. No athlete ever worked harder for a coveted prize than Mercedes, and it was not easy for her. She began to put into practice the little Carmelite saint's "Little Way of confidence and love."

Even with the best of care, Mercedes grew weaker as the disease progressed. The day finally arrived when the doctors said at most she might live only a few days, perhaps only a few hours. After Sister Margarita María told her that she would be going to heaven very, very soon, Mercedes wanted to prepare herself for this final journey. She didn't want anyone other than the Sisters or a priest around her. The Sisters, seeing how weak she had become and knowing that she could die quickly, asked the priest from the local parish to give her the Last Sacraments. After anointing her, he gave her Holy Communion.

While she made her thanksgiving after Communion, the priest and the Sisters stood at her bedside, praying quietly. Suddenly she opened her eyes, looked about, and said, "What happened? Our Lord didn't take me." She thought she was going to heaven immediately.

Mercedes lived that day and through the night. The next day was Sunday and the sixth anniversary of the canonization of the Little Flower. A Jesuit priest, Father Gerald Leahy, had come from Los Angeles to celebrate Mass and distribute Holy Communion. Again Mercedes was able to receive Our Lord.

As this was the first time that Father Leahy had come to Santa Teresita, he didn't know any of the patients, but when he was leaving, he remarked to Sister Margarita María that he would like to return and talk to that little saint.

Later in the day, Mercedes said to Mother Mary of the Eucharist, "I can't see anymore."

"Don't be concerned," she replied. "You are going to be in heaven soon." She asked for the crucifix that a friend had given her. Mercedes was so weak that she had to grasp it with both hands, and then Mother Mary had to help her raise it to her lips to kiss it.

Mercedes whispered softly, "Dear God, I love You with my whole heart. Dear God, I want to die loving You."

Mercedes was the first patient to die at Santa Teresita.

Rosario, who was a little older than the other patients, thought deeply about everything she was observing. Little by little, she also began to respond to the Sisters' kindnesses.

Although Rosario's transfer records indicated that she had been baptized a Catholic, she knew nothing about her religion. When she arrived at Santa Teresita, religion was the last thing on her mind. But as she watched the Sisters and experienced their love, she understood that it was their Catholic Faith put into practice that made them different, made them happy, made the sanatorium different, and her interest was piqued.

She began to pray. Suffering took on new meaning. A very real change was taking place in her. The bitterness and sadness so noticeable when she had been admitted were gone. She asked if she might receive her First Holy Communion. The Sisters arranged everything to make it a memorable and beautiful occasion for her. On September 24, 1930, only three weeks after she had been lifted from the ambulance, Rosario made her First Holy Communion.

Another young patient wrote the following in her journal.

A month has gone by since I came here. Such contentment I feel both in body and soul. What great kindness, patience, good care, and most of all love the Sisters show us! With so much happiness we seem to forget our sickness.

On early Sunday morning, just when the sun tips the orange groves, you can hear the Sisters' voices singing beautiful hymns, which stirs your heart and encourages you to keep on fighting for your health and love of God.

There were many sick girls, however, who were not as well prepared for death, and the Sisters paired them up with other girls who had faith. In this way, the girls themselves prepared each other for paradise.

That is what happened to Jenny Gifford, a very beautiful, blue-eyed girl of seventeen who had already studied two years at the university. She majored in the different philosophies and had read the works of Russian authors. When Sister Margarita María asked her religion upon admission, Jenny answered with enthusiasm, "Agnostic!"

IN THE FACE OF DARKNESS

Jenny arrived at Santa Teresita as a terminal case, knowing she was going to die. She had an active, hard courage born from desperation. Her roommate in the cottage was Belia, a gentle girl of deep faith with warm love and understanding flowing from her faith. Each morning Belia received Holy Communion and silently prayed for Jenny. Sister Genevieve, a Dominican nun dying of tuberculosis in the room next to theirs, was also praying for Jenny.

In December, Jenny asked to meet with the priest. "I don't want to die like this, Father. I'd better try some religion."

Belia, who was in the next bed, smiled and reached her hand across the aisle to Jenny, whispering gently, "You don't try religion, Jenny. You humbly ask your Father God for it." And that is what Jenny did. In ten lessons from Father Carlos, who visited Santa Teresita from time to time to minister to the girls, she had a clear picture of the Faith. On Holy Thursday she was wheeled into the chapel to make her First Holy Communion. It was the first time she had ever been in a Catholic chapel.

"What brought you into the Faith, Jenny?" one of the other girls asked her.

Jenny replied, "Two things: the example and kindness of my roommate, Belia, and the heroism of Sister Genevieve. You see, the walls between our two rooms are so thin that during the night when I wasn't able to sleep, I could hear Sister Genevieve, who wasn't sleeping either, praying softly, saying over and over again, 'Jesus, mercy!' and 'Jesus, I love You!' She suffered so much, yet never complained. And she spoke so beautifully of her approaching death. Only a Catholic can die like that. That is why I wanted to be one." She was a daily communicant from her First Holy Communion until the day of her death, less than a month later.

Primorosas

Sister Margarita María called the girls *primorosas* to acknowledge their beauty and dignity. A *primorosa* was poised and filled with grace, self-worth, dignity, and self-respect. This endearment was just what the girls needed, and they loved it.

Meanwhile, Mother Luisita began using her code more frequently, and her words became briefer and more guarded.

The second wave of persecution had arrived.

Chapter 28

The Second Wave

*If you look for God, everything will be fine, but if
you're looking for yourself, everything is lost.*

—Letter to Sister Margarita María, 1934

In the midst of the spiritual renewal surging through Mexico after
the peace accord, a typhoid epidemic broke out in Atotonilco
in 1930. Sister Angela of the Cross was in charge of patient care
and, having become infected with the contagious disease, was
the first of the Carmelite Sisters to die. Sister Carmen, who had
been with Sister Angela during her last days, shared her final
moments with Mother Luisita. "Mother, I'm sorry to have to tell
you that our beautiful Sister Angela died," Sister Carmen said.

"Please tell me all the details," Mother Luisita replied, bracing
herself to remain strong.

"Mother, I watched Sister Angela as she overcame the repug-
nance she felt in the midst of so much misery as she ministered
to these very sick people. She had offered to prepare and dress
a victim for burial, Mother, but as she was lifting the corpse, it
expelled a horrible black, pestilent vomit that covered her. She
was bathed in it and, although she cleansed herself immediately,

she became infected. Only fourteen days later, she died with complete serenity and joy.

"Mother, she was heroic. Right before she lost consciousness, she was very enthusiastic about the idea of going to heaven. She died on March 6. I wish you could have been there, Mother. I wish you could have seen. There were so many lilies in the convent garden when she died that we covered her body with them. Our Sister Angela was our last patient to die. Almost all the other patients are recovering at this point."

Mother dabbed her wet face with her handkerchief and then began the traditional Catholic requiem prayer. "Eternal rest grant unto her, O Lord." Sister Carmen answered, "And may perpetual light shine upon her. May her soul and the souls of all the faithful departed rest in peace. Amen."

Shortly after this epidemic, the next phase of the persecution foreseen by Archbishop Orozco y Jiménez catapulted from state to state. It began in Veracruz when Governor Adalberto Tejeda passed a law based on an overlooked clause of Article 130 of the Mexican constitution. The article declared that each state in Mexico had the right through its legislature to determine the number of priests in the state "based on the needs of the people."

Tejeda turned this clause into a lethal weapon. There were 1,100,000 people in his state of Veracruz, and he proceeded to enact through his submissive legislature a law that allowed only one priest for every 100,000 people. That came out to only 11 priests for the entire state of Veracruz.

The same thing happened in the federal district that included Mexico City. Their new law stated that there would be only 25 priests for the 1,500,000 Catholics, and they had to be approved by the governor, not by the archbishop.

The movement spread like wildfire. To protest this incredible injustice, on December 23, 1931, Archbishop Díaz addressed an open letter to the president of Mexico regarding the situation. Lawyers drew up petitions, which the people circulated. All of these efforts were in vain.

Mother Luisita told everyone, "I can't get our dear priests out of my mind. Pray for them, my Sisters. Pray for them."[27]

Several months later, in October 1932, permission was given to establish a United States province of the community, the Province of Saint Raphael. This made the community international. Mother Mary of the Eucharist was named provincial superior, and Sister Margarita María was the provincial vicar.

Mother Luisita was well aware that these vital steps forward were an affirmation by the Church that her new community and its mission were both on target and accepted by the Church. This was a huge blessing and a profound consolation.

Sitting before the Blessed Sacrament, she prayed, "Thank You, my Lord and Master, for your faithfulness. Great is Your faithfulness." Closing her eyes, she heard nothing except the spring raindrops falling slowly and gracefully on the ground outside the chapel window as she remained still in the Eucharistic Presence.

---

[27] In 1926, there were 4,500 priests in Mexico. In 1934, there were only 334 priests, and by 1935, 17 states had no priest at all. Parsons, *Mexican Martyrdom*, 163; Ramón Eduardo Ruiz, *Triumphs and Tragedy: A History of the Mexican People* (New York: W. W. Norton, 1993), 393.

Chapter 29

The Catacombs of Jalisco

*Let God mold your soul in whatever way is most pleasing to
Him. Try to be at peace within your soul, freeing yourself
and letting yourself be guided by your spiritual director.*

—Undated letter to Sister Teresita
during the religious persecution

In 1932, the Mexican government began offering a reward for
accusations against people involved in any religious activity
whatsoever. The Sisters had been living in the house on Calle
Libertad for a year without any disturbance, but in early October, rumors began to spread that the government was cracking
down on communities of religious Sisters and flushing them out
of their hiding places.

Now the spies began lingering on street corners near their
house, taking long drags on their cigarettes, and watching, always watching. Recently, the spies had arrested the Sisters of the
Sacred Heart of Jesus. They were still in prison.

As the situation escalated, Mother Luisita called Mother
Socorro, the directress of novices, and Sister Elena aside and
told them, "Go to the chancery office and ask Monsignor Anaya
what answer we should give if we are discovered."

The two understood right away the gravity of the situation. Later that morning, they walked to his office.

"Sisters, what can I do for you today?"

"Monsignor, we don't know what to do. Mother Luisita asked us to come to you for advice. Should we identify ourselves as religious Sisters if we are interrogated by the police? What should we say?" Lips pursed, they watched him intensely.

He turned slowly toward the window, stood there looking out for about a minute, and then replied, "Yes, Sisters. Yes. Each one should identify herself as a consecrated woman, a religious Sister. Do not be afraid. The Holy Spirit will answer for you. Remember, Sisters, the martyrs never prepared their answers, did they?"

They could hardly believe that after the first wave of the persecution in the 1920s, it would come to this in the 1930s — that they might really become martyrs. They were stunned by his answer as reality began to sink in. Police? Martyrdom? Mother Socorro's hands shook, and her voice trembled as she barely squeaked out, "Thank you, Monsignor, I'll tell Mother what you have told us. May we have your blessing, please?" They knelt before him, and he blessed them.

As soon as they entered the house, they found Mother Luisita and relayed Monsignor Anaya's message. She received the news solemnly. Outwardly her serenity encouraged the other Sisters; interiorly she, too, was trembling. When the Sisters left the room, she walked to the chapel and poured out her heart to Our Lord in prayer, remaining there for several hours, still as a statue.

On October 22, 1932, as Sister Elena was on her way to morning prayers, she looked out the window and noticed a man standing nonchalantly at an intersection two short blocks from their current house.

"Mother Socorro, look at the man on the corner."

Through a small opening, she was able to observe the man on the corner.

"All right," Mother Socorro replied, "We will all take turns watching the street from the crack in the window." She pointed at the hole, "Look over here. See? This crack."

Sister Elena was still peering through the crack in the window when she added, "Sisters, you know what? I recognize this spy. He is the father of one of our students. I think we can trust him to let us escape." With the hope that he would make it easier for them to escape, they began to dismantle the altar, send the sacred vessels and other religious items to neighboring houses, and consume all the consecrated hosts.

The Sisters were just beginning their breakfast when Monsignor Anaya telephoned, ordering them to leave the house immediately. They began to leave two by two with the novices exiting first through the garage. Thanks to the friendly spy, several Sisters were able to leave at intervals. Then, as the last postulant was leaving, a different man stopped her and the rest of the community and ordered them to go back into the house. The detained Sisters went back inside and sat down on a bench close to the door.

It wasn't until five o'clock in the afternoon that government officials arrived to make their investigation. Sisters Socorro, Elena, Carmen Teresa, María Asunción, and the postulant were still sitting on the bench. No law prohibited illegal search and seizure, so the officials took whatever objects they wanted. The police then escorted the five Sisters to the police station.

"Here, take this mat, and you can have it while you are here," one of the officers snarled as he threw a mat at the Sisters. But the Sisters wouldn't use it.

Sister Carmen whispered, "How can we lie on a mat in this place? Look at these men. They are all drunk. Be on your guard!"

They remained right there for two entire days. Saturday night they were transferred to Escobedo Prison without a hearing and placed in a cell with other women.

"What are you here for?" one of the women asked.

"We are Carmelite Sisters, and we are here because of our faith."

The women looked at each other and began to laugh softly.

"Why are you here?" the postulant asked. "Well, Sisters, it's like this. You've landed in a cell with prostitutes," one of the older prostitutes answered.

They stopped laughing. A young woman, perhaps twenty-five years of age, stepped forward and said, "Welcome, Sisters. I went to Catholic school. Some of my friends here are afraid of you, but I'm not afraid. Sisters, we could use some prayer in this cell."

"Will you pray with us?" one of the women asked.

Mother Socorro answered, "Yes, of course, that's exactly what we need to do," and they began praying the Rosary.

A little later, a guard came, drawn by the beautiful singing coming from one of the cells. "Well, will you look at that? Nuns and prostitutes praying together! Ha!" He gave a low guttural laugh. "Well, I never thought I'd see this here."

A voice yelled from down the hallway, "Shut up! Let the nuns pray. They should pray for you too, no?"

So the praying and singing resumed, and soon male voices down the hallway prayed with them, even joining in the hymns.

∞

"Psst. Over here." A voice was coming from the window. A large, very thin, covered basket containing food items was being slipped sideways through the vertical bars. One of the prostitutes got it and gave it to the Sisters.

"I'm pretty sure this is for you. Nobody has ever given us a basket, right, girls?" And the women just laughed.

"Then you've been in jail before?" asked the postulant.

"I can't count how many times," one of the women replied, "but they don't keep us very long."

The following morning, Holy Communion was brought to them. Everything about this event was a secret. The Sisters didn't even know who performed this great charity.

On their fifth day in custody, the five Carmelites were fingerprinted and then released. As they were leaving, the warden said, "Sisters, wait a moment. There's something I want to tell you. I would like to express to you my regret that you had to spend five days here. I want to compliment you because during your incarceration, our jail has had the first semblance of order since I've worked here."

When they returned to the house, they asked about the food basket, but they were never able to discover the source of the food or how the Eucharist had been brought to them twice during their captivity.

The five Sisters did learn, however, that Mother Luisita had never stopped praying while they were in jail and that she had been determined to take all the steps possible to obtain their prompt release. She had contacted Victor Gonzalez Luna, a lawyer and dear friend of the community. His intervention and the fact that one of the Sisters had a high-ranking official in her family were the main reasons they were freed after only five days.

After that, the police intensified their search for Mother Luisita. Forced into hiding, she immediately sequestered herself at an undisclosed place. From there she wrote a letter to Mother Mary of the Eucharist in the United States filled with coded words that showed the extreme danger. That night, as she lay awake praying, she told Our Lord: *We're all in Your hands, my Lord. There is no better place that we could be, because we trust You with all our hearts.*

They were now submerged in the second wave of the persecution.

A complete change in the schools' curricula was the next item on the government's agenda. Beginning in the early 1930s, the Mexican government had stepped up the momentum of methodically teaching more and more socialism in its public schools. With the election of General Lázaro Cárdenas as president of the Republic of Mexico in 1934, the articles of the 1917 constitution were finally fully enforced.

Cárdenas was the handpicked candidate of Plutarco Calles and carried his laws a step further. In the beginning, teachers were told that the new socialist education would exclude all religion, fanaticism, and prejudice. Shortly thereafter, all private schools that did not teach socialism were declared unconstitutional and were closed. Finally, the socialist curriculum was implemented in its entirety, with the goal of graduating students who would think and act like socialists.[28] "We must enter and take possession of the mind of childhood, the mind of youth," said Calles.[29]

---

[28] The stories on the following pages are from Parsons, *Mexican Martyrdom*, chap. 19.

[29] Quoted in George Neumayr, "The 'Private Idea' of Parental Rights," *Crisis Magazine*, April 11, 2013, https://www.crisis-magazine.com/2013/the-private-idea-of-parental-rights.

The Catacombs of Jalisco

In Guadalajara, in a single day, eighty-six schools closed, affecting tens of thousands of students. The teachers who remained in the schools, public or private, were forced to take an oath that they would teach this new curriculum. Each state formed its own oath. Part of the oath in one state included the following words and is representative of all the states:

> I declare that I am an atheist, an irreconcilable enemy
> of the Catholic Church and Roman religion, and that
> I will endeavor to destroy it, detaching conscience from
> the bonds of any religious worship and that I am ready
> to fight against the clergy anywhere and wherever it will
> be necessary.[30]

One would think that things couldn't get worse, but they did. Mother Luisita heard the stories as they were passed from person to person and then from town to town. She just shook her head, so refined and delicate of conscience that she couldn't even look up when she heard of the atrocities during the new sex education program being implemented in all grades.

She heard one of the Sisters sigh, "Here we go again." And Mother Luisita very softly whispered, "Yes, here we go again. Prayer, much prayer, is needed now."

The parents began coming to her, petrified with fear. All sense of decency left the socialist schools. Unrepeatable acts of indecency were performed in front of the students, and some included students. Sex education was taught in a grossly crude manner even to kindergartners.

---

[30] The oath was ordered by President Cárdenas in December 1935 and was required to be taken by all teachers in both public and private schools. Parsons, *Mexican Martyrdom*, 233.

IN THE FACE OF DARKNESS

One of the parents told Mother Luisita, "In one state, when a mother of a girl heard what occurred that day in school, she got out her husband's revolver, walked to the school, asked the teacher to step outside the classroom, and shot her dead."

Another parent came soon after with stories of how whole towns rose against a school. She described how the people got together with sticks and stones and showed up at the school. The teacher was with the mayor of the town, discussing the new curriculum. When they heard the mob outside, they scurried up to the roof. The townspeople took turns guarding the school, leaving the two stranded on the roof for two days and two nights without shelter or water.

About this same time, Mother Luisita's kidney condition worsened, and she experienced her first attack of uremia. Although no one said it aloud, the Sisters were sure that bearing with these aberrations was greatly affecting her health.

She encouraged the Sisters as often as she could, often sending little scraps of paper to the various hiding places.

Sursum corda! Lift up your hearts!

Or she wrote encouraging notes and letters.

> Don't feel alone, because you're not. Our Lord in the Blessed Sacrament wants to be your Confidante, your Friend, and your Consoler. He wants to fill your soul with His love. Perhaps that's why He is making you feel the emptiness of creatures.
>
> How good our God is, and by how many different paths He leads souls! Don't doubt it. You've been very dear to

Him and it's only natural that He will be jealous with those souls He loves so much. He wants you all for Himself.

Mother Luisita discreetly made her silent walks to visit the homes where novices were hiding. One group was sequestered in the house of a very virtuous widow, Doña Catarina Oro de Hernández. Mother told the novices that Doña Catarina was a valiant woman who was not afraid of hardships. So many novices were living in her home that they had to sleep on borrowed sacks thrown on the floor. The best bed this kind lady could find for Mother Luisita in her home was her bathtub, so Mother slept there.

The Sisters were living in very trying times. In April 1935, Mother Luisita traveled to the United States. While she was in Los Angeles, she became very ill. Her neck and face were extremely swollen. She had been battling a glandular infection in her neck, and after she was in California for a few weeks, it began to worsen. The Sisters contacted Doctor Steven McAtee, their physician.

He met Mother at the hospital early the following morning. Doctor Holleran, a highly respected surgeon, also examined her. He ordered an immediate operation.

Surgery was performed the following day. Doctor Holleran told Mother Margarita María, who was the local superior at Santa Teresita, of Mother Luisita's grave condition.

"Sister, Mother suffers from advanced septicemia. She has no longer than two years to live, and we are placing her in isolation until the infection is gone. I must tell you that this is the worst infection I have seen in my career as a physician."

Mother Luisita ended up in a room in the hospital basement, isolated from the other patients. This was the standard protocol at Queen of Angels Hospital in the 1930s.

IN THE FACE OF DARKNESS

Mother Luisita remained in the United States longer than she had originally planned to allow more time for recuperation following her surgery. When she returned to Mexico, the condition of the country was about the same.

In August 1935, the family came under attack.

The new law stated that the government would confiscate any building, including a family's home, if any type of religious activity whatsoever was carried out within that home, even if the supposed actions were inferred or implied.

Then, quite unexpectedly, in 1936, President Cárdenas adopted a more conciliatory policy regarding religion. This was a huge step on the part of the Mexican government in burying the hatchet that had been wielded for ten years against the Mexican Catholic population. The *New York Times* ran an article, quoting Cárdenas's words:

> The government will not commit the error of previous administrations by considering the religious question as a problem preeminent to other issues involved in the national program. Antireligious campaigns would only result in further resistance and definitely postpone economic revival.[31]

This major policy change brought hope to the hearts of the Carmelite Sisters in Mexico. Mother Luisita forged ahead, opening three more schools in 1936—Jamay, Jalisco; Mexticacán, Jalisco; and Santo Tomás de los Plátanos in the state of Mexico.

---

[31] J. Lloyd Mecham, *Church and State in Latin America: A History of Politico-Ecclesiastical Relations* (Chapel Hill: University of North Carolina Press, 1934), 409, citing a *New York Times* article of March 31, 1936.

The Catacombs of Jalisco

Nine houses. Seven in Mexico and two in the United States, Los Angeles and Duarte. A priest had told her many years ago that she would not die until seven houses were established. She smiled as she remembered his words.

Chapter 30

The Fragrance of Roses

We thought about the first miracle of Our Lord, which He worked through the intercession of Our Lady. This meditation made me reflect that if I would only pray the way I should, and beg for the protection of our Blessed Mother, my soul would be transformed from bad to good, from a life of superficiality to one of fruitfulness, and from one of dissipation to one of continuous prayer.

—From the spiritual notes of Mother Luisita

"Not many steps left, Mother. You can do it," coached the younger Sisters, leading Mother Luisita to the front of the room.

No answer.

All her strength went into just making it down the aisle. With every step, flashes of pain shot through Mother's legs, and her tired heart pumped mightily to move her slowly along to her destination. For a while now, she had struggled just to keep going. Her heart condition was worsening.

With tightly closed lips, and two of the Sisters assisting her, she slowly put one foot in front of the other on her journey to the front of the room.

She didn't have to kneel, but she wanted to. She willed herself to her knees. The Very Reverend Father Alejandro Navarro, vicar-general of the Archdiocese of Guadalajara, was presiding, and Mother Luisita had just been reelected as the superior general of the Carmelite Sisters.

It was July 12, 1936, and after all these years of waiting, the first ordinary general chapter of the new community was finally taking place in Guadalajara.[32] This was their first official election.

Kneeling before the vicar-general, she begged to be released from her responsibility as superior general. She looked up at him.

Gently shaking his head no, he looked directly at her and said, "Mother Luisita, as long as you live, you shall be the superior general. This is the decision of the chapter."

She could feel tiredness in her bones. She swallowed hard, looked back at him, and said, "Yes, Your Excellency. I accept."

She walked a longer, more difficult journey to the chancery office in downtown Guadalajara to see Archbishop José Garibi Rivera. He had succeeded Archbishop Orozco y Jiménez after his death on February 18, 1936, only five months earlier.

Step by painful step, she made her way to his office. She had determined to let him know personally of the results of the election and to ask him to confirm her as the newly reelected superior general and to bless the congregation.

The new archbishop understood the effort it had taken her to reach his office. As she entered the room, he stood up and walked toward the seriously ill seventy-year-old woman, understanding that she wouldn't be with them much longer. Almost tenderly, he confirmed her in her office as superior general and blessed her and her community.

---

[32] A general chapter is a meeting required by the canon law of the Catholic Church for all religious communities in the Church for elections and decision-making.

And life went on.

Three months later, on October 15, 1936, a knock on the door surprised the Sisters living in the house on Calle Mezquitán in Guadalajara. They opened the door to receive an official, hand-delivered letter from the chancery office. It said, "LEAVE IMMEDIATELY! YOU ARE IN IMMEDIATE DANGER!" The letter was from the vicar-general for religious, who ordered them to leave the house straightaway and disperse to houses of friends. They followed these orders at once.

So it happened that Mother Luisita and her community moved again, this time to Calle Garibaldi no. 761, a very small house with poor accommodations. Mother Carmen gasped and exclaimed, "Mother, this awful house looks like a sepulcher!"

With a wry smile, Mother Luisita just shook her head. She answered, "It doesn't matter. It doesn't matter. From this sepulcher to heaven, but what will you Sisters do with a dead body in this small house?" she asked, alluding to her own departure from this world.

She recalled the many homes that had offered her Sisters hospitality over the years. Years ago, they moved to a home on Independence Street, which they named "the House of Straits" because of the narrowness of its corridors. Later that same year, they moved to another residence on the same street. They called it "the House of Bedbugs" because of the huge insect population. It had once served as a chicken coop.

Mother Luisita loved the little "Sepulcher House" because it was so close to the parish church, Holy Name of Jesus. She loved the fact that Conchita Hernández, Mother Margarita María's mother, lived next door. Most of all, she loved that the home had an oratory — the dining room — and that the Blessed Sacrament was hidden there. She loved to sit in the lovely, though small, inside patio, and when she was too ill to get out of bed, she could see the patio from her bed.

But, if truth be told, it was an inadequate house for them. It was very poor, very small, and with very few rooms.

"I would like all the Sisters to come to Guadalajara with me this Christmas." Mother Luisita knew that this Christmas would be her last, and so did everyone else.

Christmas was just around the corner, and her illness was causing her to waste away little by little. One day, when Mother Mary was at her bedside, Mother Luisita looked up at her and said, "I am experiencing something I have never felt before."

"What? Tell me." Mother Mary put down the book she was reading.

Mother Luisita shook her head. "I can't explain it."

A few days later, she confided again to Mother Mary. "I feel so many things, but I don't want to worry you."

"Tell me about it."

"No, I can't explain it."

She never brought up this subject again.

Sister Dolores of Jesus took her turn to sit by Mother's bedside while she was sewing a crown of flowers to be worn by Sister Catalina of the Cross at the ceremony of her upcoming perpetual vows.

Mother Luisita looked up. "My daughter, are you almost finished with my crown?"

Sister Dolores replied, "Your crown? How about that! This crown won't fit you, Mother."

"Try it," Mother said.

Sister Dolores placed the crown on Mother's head. To her surprise, with the sewing of only two more flowers the crown would fit perfectly.

Mother said, "Please make sure that a crown is made for my death."

Sister Dolores looked down and sighed. Looking back up, she turned toward Mother Luisita, took her hand, and said, "Yes, but you must let me know ahead of time when this will happen!"

"My daughter," Mother replied, "I am telling you."

Feeling that her life in this world was coming to an end, Mother asked to speak with Archbishop José Garibi Rivera. Since he was out of the city, the vicar for religious, Don Alejandro Navarro, came to her bedside.

"I place my work and my congregation into your hands," she told him.

After this surrender, if a Sister asked any permission or brought up any issue that needed guidance, Mother Luisita simply shook her head and replied firmly, "I have already surrendered all."

A few days later, she asked Mother Carmen of Jesus, "My daughter, tell me something that will sweeten my soul." To Mother Teresa of Jesus she asked, "Please read something to me that will help me die a holy death." Her physical condition was worsening.

One of the younger Sisters, Sister Patrocinio, who had made her vows only a year and a half before, became Mother Luisita's companion during these final months.

"Sister Patrocinio, I would like you to stay with me. I am going to need help. I would like you to be the one."

Since that time, Sister Patrocinio stayed with her, tending to the treatment of Mother Luisita's nasal passages, filled with infection as a consequence of her diabetes. Sister Patrocinio would sit quietly for hours in the adjoining room, patiently waiting for the little bell to ring, and then she would go to Mother Luisita's room to alleviate the pain the infection caused.

IN THE FACE OF DARKNESS

On February 9, Father José Refugio Huerta, S.J., came to see her and administered the Sacrament of the Sick.

On Ash Wednesday, February 10, Mother Luisita seemed to be able to hear the ringing of the parish bells. About 10:00 a.m., an unknown priest arrived at the house and said, "I know there is a sick person here, and I wonder if she wants to receive Holy Communion."

"Mother, Our Lord is here. Do you want to receive Holy Communion?" Mother nodded, lifted her head, and received Our Lord in the Holy Eucharist for the last time.

Later she asked, "Please call Mother Mary. I would like to see her."

Mother Mary hurried to her little alcove. "Here I am, Mother. I will stay and pray with you."

Father Feliciano Leal, S.J., arrived to assist her. He held Mother's hand up and helped her make the Sign of the Cross as he named each of her foundations to her.

Father Eduardo Huerta, pastor of the Church of the Holy Name, also came to pray. Leaning close to her, he whispered, "Our Lord has placed you on the Cross, but from it you will fly to heaven."

Archbishop José Garibi Rivera came by unexpectedly. Mother Luisita recognized his voice when he called her name and tried to get on her knees but was too weak. He whispered in her ear, "May Your will be done on earth as it is in heaven" and continued to prepare her for a happy death.

After he left the house, he said that a priest would be sent to give the blessing of the Most Blessed Sacrament at the moment of her death and offer the Holy Sacrifice of the Mass.

That priest, Father Modesto Sánchez, soon arrived to accompany her last moments at the request of the archbishop. She was already unconscious. Her breathing was labored, and her eyes were closed. Father Sánchez made himself comfortable on the sofa a short distance from her bed. Then he waited.

Hours slipped by.

Between three and four o'clock in the morning, Father Sánchez noticed that Mother's breathing began to decrease. He went to the oratory and returned with the Most Blessed Sacrament in the small reliquary, which had been hidden there.

As the Angelus bells were ringing, he blessed her with the Blessed Sacrament and commended her soul to God. She sighed a final breath peacefully at five o'clock.

She looked as if she had just fallen asleep.

According to the diagnoses of Doctor Luis Arechiga, her agony was excruciating because of her medical complications: diabetes, arteriosclerosis, active inflammation of the liver, pulmonary congestion, and uremia.

Mother Luisita always had a rosary in her hand during her illness. After she died, it was found under her body.

The Sisters improvised an altar, and there, in the same room, Father Sánchez celebrated Holy Mass for her. It was early morning on February 11, 1937, the feast of Our Lady of Lourdes.

Later in the morning, the vicar-general for religious arrived, and when he saw the great number of people, he quietly told everyone to remain kneeling before Mother's remains.

"How did the news of her death spread so quickly — like wildfire?" the Sisters asked each other. Hour after hour, people came to touch objects of devotion to her body. They prayed and asked for her intercession.

Some of the Sisters stayed all night in the room with her body, keeping vigil. The following morning, Sister Paulina related what she experienced during her vigil. "There was a very disagreeable odor permeating the whole room when I first entered—from that awful infection in her nose. Around two o'clock in the morning, when I was still on my knees, I noticed a pleasant fragrance. It was the aroma of roses. Fresh roses. The bad smell had gone. When I turned to look at her, I found that her face had changed. It was different somehow. As I got closer, her face was fuller. Rosy. Like velvet. It was more beautiful than ever."

Little whispers. "I saw that, too."

"Yes, that's the way she looked."

Sister Paulina turned and nodded. "I didn't want to say anything about what happened, but others who were there had the same impression I experienced."

Priests from different cities arrived to celebrate Mass before Mother's body. Four Masses were celebrated in the room where she lay—two the day she died and two more in the early morning the day after her death.

The funeral Mass was held on February 12 at the Church of the Holy Name of Jesus, even though it was still a crime to have a Christian burial in Mexico. Father Alberto Urdanivia, S.J., who knew Mother Luisita and her community so well, spoke to those present. "Someday you will have to write everything about Mother Luisita's life and work—and that day is today!"

Mother Luisita was buried in the holy habit of the Carmelite Order with Sister Catalina's crown of flowers on her head.

Her face was glowing, and she seemed to be asleep.

Epilogue

The day after Mother Luisita's funeral, the police became suspicious when they saw so many people walking into the house. To evade capture, the Sisters who were present climbed quickly onto the roof of the Garibaldi house and then leapt onto the roof of Conchita Hernandez's house next door, just as the police knocked on the front door. Thanks be to God, they all made it and were not discovered.

Blessed Ezequiel and Blessed Salvador Huerta were martyred on April 3, 1927, after being tortured. They were beatified in 2005 by Pope Benedict XVI. They never divulged the whereabouts of their priest brothers Fathers José Refugio and Eduardo Huerta, whom the government wanted to find and kill.

Blessed Pedro Heriz, O.C.D., Mother Luisita's adviser and confidant, was martyred in Spain in November 1936 and beatified on October 13, 2013, by Pope Francis.

In 1938, a year after Mother Luisita's death, the Carmelite Sisters in California were no longer classified as refugees.

That same year, 1938, the California Department of Health commended Santa Teresita as "one of the loveliest sanatoria in the United States." (Letter from State of California Department of Public Health, October 26, 1938. The name Santa Teresita Rest Home had been changed to Santa Teresita Sanatorium in 1937.)

On April 25, 1949, Mother Luisita's community was given the *Decretum Laudi* (Decree of Praise) by the Catholic Church. The *Decretum Laudis* is the official measure with which the Holy See grants to institutes of consecrated life and societies of apostolic life the recognition of ecclesiastical institution of pontifical right—that is, not under the authority of the bishop, but directly responsible to the Holy See.

On June 18, 1981, in the chapter hall of the cathedral church in Guadalajara, the ceremony of the opening process of the beatification of Mother Luisita took place.

On February 2, 1983, the California province was raised to the status of an autonomous institute of pontifical right with the name the Carmelite Sisters of the Most Sacred Heart of Los Angeles.

On September 21, 1992, President Carlos Salinas of Mexico reestablished full diplomatic relations with the Vatican after a break of more than 130 years, completing a reconciliation based on the government's restoration of legal rights to religious groups earlier in 1992. The government ratified its informal policy of not enforcing most legal controls on religious groups by, among other things, granting religious groups legal status, conceding them limited property rights, and lifting restrictions on the number of priests in the country.

On July 1, 2000, Mother Luisita was declared Venerable by Pope Saint John Paul II.

Today, Mother Luisita's two communities, the Carmelite Sisters of the Most Sacred Heart of Los Angeles and the Carmelite Sisters of the Sacred Heart of Mexico continue to make God's love visible throughout the United States, from Florida to California. They bring God's love not only to the people of the United States and Mexico but also to the people of Central and South America, the Philippines, and Cambodia.

Mother Luisita's communities have a collection of favors, graces, and healings attributed to the intercession of Mother Luisita. There are medical cases being studied as the needed miracles for her beatification at the time of the writing of this book (2018).

The members of the de la Peña family continue the family tradition of getting together once a year on the feast of Saint Joseph, a tradition begun by Mother Luisita's father, Don Epigmenio de la Peña, and carried on by his children and their descendants.

Mother Luisita's remains are located in a side chapel at the motherhouse of the Carmelite Sisters of the Sacred Heart of Mexico in Atotonilco el Alto, Jalisco. People visit this beautiful chapel to pray by her remains.

Appendices

My Farewell to My Carmelite Daughters

Above all, I wish to express my gratitude and give you my thanks for the submission, respect, and affection that you have shown toward her whom God Our Lord gave you to be your Mother. I congratulate you for this, because there is no other way for good religious to be. I ask you to conduct yourselves in this manner with my successors, because the success and growth of the Community depend on it.

I ask each of you to forgive me for whatever I have made you suffer and for the bad example I may have given you, which I implore you not to follow.

From my heart, I earnestly ask you that, for the love of God Our Lord, you be very united and treat one another as if everything depended on you individually for this unity. Help one another and tolerate one another's faults with patience.

Fervently resolve to obey your superiors, for it is a sure means to your sanctification. It will benefit you to do all of your works and endure whatever sufferings God Our Lord sends you, solely for the love of Him and for His greater honor and glory. Work diligently for children and for the sick. May all your conversations engender love of the Most Blessed Sacrament and our most Blessed Mother.

The legacy I leave to the Congregation is the inheritance I have received. It is to be used for the novitiate house in Guadalajara, and for the needy houses of the Community, each of which has an equal right in case of need. When possible, the superior, along with her council, will distribute allowances to the houses according to the necessity of each. These funds are to be maintained permanently.

May God Our Lord bless you.

María Luisa Josefa of the Most Blessed Sacrament, O.C.D.
Guadalajara, Jalisco, December 22, 1934

Appendix B

The Cause

The official petition to introduce the Cause of Mother Maria Luisa Josefa of the Most Blessed Sacrament (Mother Luisita) was sent to the chancery of the Archdiocese of Guadalajara, on November 11, 1968. Father Finian Monahan, O.C.D., superior general of the Discalced Carmelites, authorized Father Simeón Fernández to be the postulator in charge of the Cause.

At the completion of the preliminary works assigned by the postulator of the Cause and fulfilled under his guidance, the corresponding procedures were initiated in Rome in the Congregation for the Cause of the Saints.

During the Synod on the Family in 1980, Cardinal Pietro Palazzini, prefect of the Congregation for the Causes of the Saints, in two synodal interventions, mentioned the Servant of God, underlining the introduction of her Cause.

> There are other causes to be introduced, and they concern the Servant of God, María Luisa de la Peña Rojas, also Mexican, of the Diocese of Guadalajara, Foundress of the Congregation of the Carmelite Sisters of the Sacred Heart (1866–1937). In the world María Luisa de la Peña Rojas received the Sacrament of Matrimony at 16 years of

age. She had no children and together with her husband dedicated herself to the works of charity. After becoming a widow she joined the Order of Carmel and founded a new Religious Congregation.

On December 12, 1980, the same cardinal prefect signed the decree of the Congregation for the Cause of the Saints, and he gave the nihil obstat for the opening of the investigation in the Diocese of Guadalajara, Mexico. On January 26, 1981, His Holiness John Paul II affirmed and confirmed the response to the Congregation for the Causes of Saints. The postulator of the Cause traveled to Guadalajara, taking the rescript with the faculties of Cardinal José Salazar López to initiate the process.

On June 14, 1981, the Edict of Introduction of the Cause was published. It was read at all the Masses in all the parishes of the Archdiocese of Guadalajara and kept in a conspicuous place for the faithful to see for one week. Everything was ready to begin.

On the feast of Corpus Christi, June 18, 1981, in the chapter hall of the cathedral church in Guadalajara, the ceremony of the opening process of the beatification of the foundress of the Carmelite Sisters of the Sacred Heart took place. The ceremony was private and very simple. Those present were the priests of the tribunal who had been named by the cardinal and his representative, Auxiliary Bishop D. Adolfo Hernández Hurtado. A good number of Sisters of the congregation were witnesses of this historic moment.

On July 1, 2000, Mother Luisita's heroic virtues were confirmed by the Church, and she was declared Venerable.[33]

---

[33] *Positio Super Virtutibus: Canonizatiois Servae Dei Maríae Aloisiae Iosephace a SS. Sacramento* (Rome: Tipografia Guerra, 1991).

The Cause

*Prayer for the Beatification of
Mother María Luisa Josefa of the Most
Blessed Sacrament (Mother Luisita)*

O Jesus in the Holy Eucharist,
King and Center of all Hearts,
look with merciful love upon
the petitions we present to You
through the intercession of Your servant,
Mother María Luisa Josefa
of the Most Blessed Sacrament.

(*Here mention your petition.*)

We humbly beseech You to glorify her
who was always such a fervent
lover of Your Sacred Heart
by granting us these favors
if they are for Your greater
honor and glory.
Amen.

Please report any graces or favors received to the superior general
of the Carmelite Sisters.

Superior General
Carmelite Sisters of the Most Sacred Heart of Los Angeles
920 East Alhambra Road, Alhambra, CA 91801
(626) 576-4910
contacts@carmelitesistersocd.com
www.carmelitesistersocd.com

Appendix C

Mother Luisita by Those Who Knew Her

Excerpts from testimonies of some persons in this book

"What was Mother Luisita to her Carmelite Sisters? She was an angel who, through her example and virtues, modeled the sweet aspect of the religious Sisters in her congregation. She spent her whole soul, her whole fortune, and also her body in the congregation she founded, which has given so much glory to God, to the Church, and to society. She was a model religious, an unblemished superior, and a reservoir of tenderness and charity for the whole world. Her main virtues were modesty, abnegation, piety, and constancy, but what was most outstanding about her is that she left in her magnificent work, her whole exquisite personality and all the sweetness of her incomparable charity."

> —Father Macario Velázquez Abarca, who was pastor in Atotonilo el Alto and received Mother Luisita's final vows in 1925 and who knew her and the members of the new community very well

"She was a friend to all the townspeople. They called her 'the heart and soul of Atotonilco.' She was kind to everybody, and each felt especially loved by her. Consequently,

IN THE FACE OF DARKNESS

Mother was a person whom everyone loved. The Sisters used to wrap Mother Luisita in a small white blanket (called a *zarapito*) when she was ill, and she was carried in a small cart [in the early days]. I was then a schoolgirl. Mother's special devotions were a great love for the Most Blessed Sacrament, the Sacred Heart, the Blessed Virgin, Saint Teresa of Jesus, and Saint John of the Cross."

—Mother Maria de la Divina Eucaristía, who was with Mother Luisita in the United States and was the first local superior of Santa Teresita

"Mother's joy always seemed to me as a gentle reflection of her pure and upright heart. Her joy was sweet, simple, gentle, modest, never ostentatious or boisterous. Her face reflected sweetness, since this was one of her characteristics. She never raised her voice. We could say we saw her laugh, but we did not hear her laugh."

—Mother Carmen of Jesus, who was one of the first Sisters to come to the United States during the persecution

"In 1928, I traveled to the United States to join the Sisters working at Saint Mary's College. The work there was very hard, and we broke many dishes. They [the Christian Brothers] even had to ask Mother to tell us not to break so many, but she said, 'Poor Sisters, they get so tired. Let them take it out of our salary.' She was very considerate, and she suffered for her daughters in Mexico, and those in the United States."

—Sister Maria del Rosario, whose photograph was taken during the smallpox epidemic and shown in the newspapers

"During the revolution, I [was assigned] to Atotonilco. We would go to see Mother Luisita and the Sisters. Our Mother was in hiding, sometimes alone or with Mother Elena de la Cruz. 'Oh, my daughter,' she would say, 'this is beyond my strength.' Fear of the persecution was very intense, very great, very great. Again she would repeat: 'My daughter, I expose you to danger. What if the troops will take one of our little Sisters?'

"From Saint Mary's I came to Los Angeles, but only just for the time it took for me to prepare to return to Mexico. When I was there, just about ready to return to Mexico, I had engraved in my mind the poverty of that little house located in front of Saint Patrick's Church, which by then already belonged to the community. I almost went crazy there, because we were in front of an emergency center, and there was noise all night long; I could not sleep. At Saint Patrick's, we did the same kind of mission work as we did in Long Beach. Soon after I left, it became a boarding school. Mother recommended we pray much in order to be able to suffer whatever would come upon us."

—Sister Maria Refugio of the Sacred Heart, who arrived with the second group of Sisters to the United States in 1927

"In Long Beach, there was a church in honor of Our Lady of Guadalupe, especially for the Mexican people. When more Sisters arrived, they dedicated themselves to serve in this mission church. They used to call us the exiled Mexican Sisters. Within six months of this apostolate in the mission church, the Protestant church building had become a laundromat because it had been abandoned by the people. Soon after, the proposal came to Mother to take us to work at Saint Mary's. We did, but then, Mother used to cry at seeing us work so hard."

—Sister Teresa of Jesus, Mother Luisita's second
cousin, who was one of the original three Sisters
to come to the United States as a refugee

"During the Cristeros' revolution, I had the good fortune to be with her, in hiding, with four other Sisters. We were 'walled in' in Don Jesús Camacho's house; and for one hour each one of us had to stand with arms extended in prayer, so that the Cristeros would win. When it was my turn, I lowered my arms very soon. Then Mother Elena told me to lift them up again, and Mother Luisita said to me, 'My daughter, I will take your place. Sit down,' and I sat down. At that time, I did not understand that this was great charity and kindness on her part, but now I see that it was heroic charity.

"What can I say of her angelic purity? One could see in her eyes, the purity of her soul. And now I can say, as did Saint John the Evangelist, 'She, who speaks, has seen it and gives testimony to the truth.' Mother Luisita's motto was 'Unite the apostolate to prayer.' She taught by example. She suffered in silence. She loved Christ and her brethren."

—Sister Margarita of Christ, who was one of
the refugee Sisters in the United States

"In Mexico, we were very poor, and we did not have any light. One night, I told her that I had not slept because I was very much afraid. She prepared some small candles and match and lighter, and she spent the whole night holding a small wire with the match lighter, which gave out light.

This she did for my sake. It seems to me that this could not have been done by anyone but a saint. On another occasion, when I arrived from school, she was writing at a little table. I sat down next to her on a small floor mat, and as I leaned on her knees, I fell asleep. When I woke up I realized that all the Sisters were in the chapel, so I told her. She told me that she had remained still so as not to wake me up. This seemed to me to be a very maternal act."

—Sister Inés of Jesus, who was one of the
refugee Sisters in the United States

Appendix D

The Code Used by Mother Luisita

Code words used in Mother's letters	Meaning
Grandfather, "Papa Panchito"	Archbishop Francisco Orozco y Jiménez
Grandfather, "Papa Juanito"	Archbishop John J. Cantwell
Workers	Aspirants to the community
The little town	Atotonilco el Alto, Jalisco
Grandfather, papa, papacito, tata, daddy	Bishop or a parish priest
Elenita's house, Socorro's house, the family	Local communities
The birth of a girl	Entrance into the congregation
To settle	To establish congregation in a given place
To train	Formation in the religious life

IN THE FACE OF DARKNESS

Code words used in Mother's letters	Meaning
Father, Helio, Jesus, Spouse, Papacito, Manuelito (which is for Emmanuel)	God or Christ
Sons of Ignatius, sons of Albert	Jesuits
Mama, mother, grand-mother, "Mama Pepa"	Mother Luisita
Father Macario Velazquez, Godfather, Maco	The pastor
Patron, sir, priest	Person in charge of an apostolate
Matrimony, marriage, to get married, espousal, feast	Profession of vows (first and final)
Grandmother, mama	Religious persecution in Mexico
Vacation, yearly outing	Spiritual Exercises or retreat
Family, little ones, cousins	Sisters in the congregation
To do another Sister's work while she is absent	To take over a Sister's duty
My uncle, or papa	Vicar-general/vicar for religious

Appendix E

Anti-Religious Articles of the
1917 Mexican Constitution

Article 27, II. Religious institutions known as churches, regardless of creed, may in no case acquire, hold, or administer real property or hold mortgages thereon; such property held at present either directly or through an intermediary shall revert to the Nation, any person whosoever being authorized to denounce any property so held. Presumptive evidence shall be sufficient to declare the denunciation well founded. Places of public worship are the property of the Nation, as represented by the Federal Government, which shall determine which of them may continue to be devoted to their present purposes. Bishoprics, rectories, seminaries, asylums, and schools belonging to religious orders, convents, or any other buildings built or intended for the administration, propagation, or teaching of a religious creed shall at once become the property of the Nation by inherent right, to be used exclusively for the public services of the Federal or State Governments, within their respective jurisdictions. All places of public worship hereafter erected shall be the property of the Nation.

Article 27: III. Public or private charitable institutions for the rendering of assistance to the needy, for scientific research, the diffusion of knowledge, mutual aid to members, or for any other lawful purpose, may not acquire more real property than actually needed for their purpose and immediately and directly devoted thereto; but they may acquire, hold, or administer mortgages on real property provided the term hereof does not exceed ten years. Under no circumstances may institutions of this kind be under the patronage, direction, administration, charge, or supervision of religious orders or institutions, or of ministers of any religious sect or of their followers, even though the former or the latter may not be in active service.

Article 130. The federal powers shall exercise the supervision required by law in matters relating to religious worship and outward ecclesiastical forms. Other authorities shall act as auxiliaries of the Federation. Congress cannot enact laws establishing or prohibiting any religion.... The law does not recognize any personality in religious groups called churches....

Ministers of denominations shall be considered as persons who practice a profession and shall be directly subject to the laws enacted on such matters.

Only the legislatures of the States shall have the power to determine the maximum number of ministers of denominations necessary for local needs.

To practice the ministry of any denomination in the United Mexican States it is necessary to be a Mexican by birth.

Ministers of denominations may never, in a public or private meeting constituting an assembly, or in acts of worship or religious propaganda, criticize the fundamental laws of the country or the authorities of the Government, specifically or generally. They shall not have an active or passive vote or the right to form associations for religious purposes.

Permission to dedicate new places of worship open to the public must be obtained from the Secretariat of Government, with previous consent of the government of the State. There must be in every church building a representative who is responsible to the authorities for compliance with the laws on religious worship in such building, and for the objects pertaining to the worship.

The representative of each church building, jointly with ten other residents of the vicinity, shall inform the municipal authorities immediately who is the person in charge of the church in question. Any change of ministry must be reported by the departing minister in person, accompanied by the new incumbent and ten other residents. The municipal authority, under penalty of removal from office and a fine of up to one thousand pesos for each violation, shall see that this provision is complied with; under the same penalty, he shall keep one registry book of church buildings and another of the representatives in charge. The municipal authority shall give notice to the Secretariat of Government, through the governor of the State, of every permit to open a new church building to the public, or of any changes among representatives in charge. Donations in the form of movable objects shall be kept in the interior of church buildings.

No privilege shall be granted or confirmed, nor shall any other step be taken which has for its purpose the validation in official courses of study, of courses pursued in establishments devoted to the professional training of ministers of religion. Any authority that violates this provision shall be criminally liable, and the privilege or step referred to shall be void and shall thereby cause the voidance of the professional degree for the attainment of which the violation of this provision was made.

IN THE FACE OF DARKNESS

Periodical publications of a religious character, whether they are such because of their program, title, or merely because of their general tendencies, may not comment on national political matters or public information on acts of the authorities of the country or of private persons directly related to the functioning of public institutions.

The formation of any kind of political group, the name of which contains any word or indication whatsoever that it is related to any religious denomination, is strictly prohibited. Meetings of a political character may not be held in places of worship.

Ministers of any denomination may not himself or through an intermediary inherit or receive any real property occupied by any association for religious propaganda or for religious or charitable purposes. Ministers of denominations are legally incapacitated as testamentary heirs of ministers of the same denomination or of any private person who is not related to them within the fourth degree.

The acquisition by private parties of personal or real property owned by the clergy or by religious organizations shall be governed by Article 27 of this Constitution.

Trials for violation of the above provisions shall never be heard before a jury.[34]

---

[34] 1917 Constitution of Mexico, posted at Latin American Studies, http://www.latinamericanstudies.org/mexico/1917-Constitution. htm.

Appendix F

The Carmelite Sisters

The Shield of the Carmelite Sisters of the Most Sacred Heart of Los Angeles

A charism defines the particular essence of an individual or religious community. The shield of the Carmelite Sisters of the Most Sacred Heart of Los Angeles is a symbolic expression of the Teresian Carmelite charism given to us through Mother Luisita, our foundress.

The center of the shield depicts a mountain symbolizing Mount Carmel in Israel, where the order was born. It also symbolizes the soul's union with God through prayer and contemplation.

IN THE FACE OF DARKNESS

The lifelong deepening and intensifying of this union with God is signified by the soul's ascent up the mountain of the Lord.

On the top of the mountain is the cross, representing the person of Jesus Christ and His redeeming death.

The Sacred Heart of Jesus at the center of the cross is in honor of our community's name. In the Eucharistic love of the Sacred Heart we discover the privileged place of encounter between the human and the divine. Christ reveals His hidden presence in the ordinary events of daily life. In our call to be contemplatives in action, we seek to encounter Him in every moment.

The spring of water flowing from the Heart of Christ in the Eucharist signifies our union with God in prayer overflowing into active works. As mentioned in our Constitutions, "Whatever work is entrusted to us flows from and is a part of our union with God" (chap. 8). Our apostolates of education, health care, and retreat work all form part of that stream as we promote a deeper spiritual life among God's people.

The three stars stand for the three spiritual traditions of the order: eremitical, prophetic, and Marian. The eremitical tradition represented in the star on the right signifies Saint Elijah, who was a solitary seeker of God. Saint Elijah encountered God in the gentle breeze of silent contemplation, which impelled him to go down from the mount to serve God with zeal and single-hearted dedication. "With zeal I have been zealous for the Lord God of hosts" (1 Kings 19:14).

The prophetic tradition represented in the star on the left signifies John the Baptist, who prepared the way for us to enter into the new covenant. By our charism, we live out this prophetic call by disposing ourselves to receive the fullness of God's grace in an ever deeper union with Him through prayer and facilitating this encounter with the Living God among His people.

The Marian tradition symbolized by the star in the center represents Mary, Star of the Sea. She is our guiding light who abides with us as we seek to live in familiarity with God and to respond as she did in complete allegiance to Jesus Christ.

The crown represents Mary as Queen and Beauty of Carmel, our model of living a hidden union with Christ in loving contemplation and fruitful service. We strive to live in docile obedience to the action of the Holy Spirit in our daily lives under her queenship.

Share the Mission

Food for the Soul... Read it. Pray it. Share it.

Carmelite Sisters of the Most Sacred Heart of Los Angeles
At the Service of Your Family

Childcare	www.haydenchildcare.com
Elementary & High School	www.holyinnocentsschlb.org (CA)
	www.stphilomenaschool.org (CA)
	https://lorettoschool.org/ (AZ)
	www.stscg.org (FL)
	www.peterandpaulcatholic.org (CO)
	www.colemancarroll.org (FL)
Retreats	www.sacredheartretreathouse.com
Independent Living for Seniors	www.avilagardens.com
Assisted Living & Skilled Nursing	www.santa-teresita.org
Skilled Nursing	www.marycrestculvercity.com

 www.carmelitesistersocd.com |  www.facebook.com/CarmeliteSisters
 www.twitter.com/CarmelitesOCD |  www.instagram.com/CarmeliteSistersOCD

Bibliography

Arquieta, Sister Piedad, O.C.D. Interview with author. Alhambra, California, November 24, 1997.

Bartoli, Lucia. Interview with author. Duarte, California, September 25, 2016.

Boudinhon, A. "Canon Law." *Catholic Encyclopedia*. New York: Robert Appleton, 1910. http://www.newadvent.org/cathen/09056a.htm.

Brenner, Anita. *The Wind That Swept Mexico*. Austin: University of Texas Press, 1971.

Caravacci, Ariadne Katherine. *Loving Kindness*. Alhambra, CA: Carmelite Sisters' Printing, 1983.

Carmelite Sisters of the Most Sacred Heart of Los Angeles. *Community Hymnbook of the Carmelite Sisters of the Most Sacred Heart of Los Angeles*. Alhambra, CA: Carmelite Sisters' Printing, 2013.

Colbert, Helenita. *The Flower of Guadalajara*. Alhambra, CA: Carmelite Sisters' Printing, 1956.

———. *To Love Me in Truth: Mother María Luisa Josefa of the Most Blessed Sacrament*. Alhambra, CA: Carmelite Sisters' Printing, 1987.

Congregation for Institutes of Consecrated Life and for Societies of Apostolic Life, *Verbi Sponsa: Instruction on the Contemplative Life and on the Enclosure of Nuns and The Code of Canon Law*. May 13, 1999. http://www.vatican.va/roman_curia/congregations/ccscrlife/documents/rc_con_ccscrlife_doc_13051999_verbi-sponsa_en.html.

Constitutions of the Carmelite Sisters of the Most Sacred Heart of Los Angeles. Alhambra, CA: Archives of the Carmelite Sisters of the Most Sacred Heart of Los Angeles, 1987.

De la Peña, Carlos Hector. *Biografía de Mi Muy Amada Tía, Luisa Josefa del Santísimo Sacramento*. Guadalajara, 1945.

Early History of the Carmelite Sisters of the Most Sacred Heart of Los Angeles: 1927–1937. Compiled by Sister Mary Jeanne Coderre, O.C.D. Alhambra, CA: Archives of the Carmelite Sisters of the Most Sacred Heart of Los Angeles.

Eschevarria, Antonio Unzueta. *Beato Pedro De San Elías: Biografía y Espistolario*. Vitoria-Gasteis: Ediciones El Carmen, 2015.

Heath, Earl. *75 Years of Progress: An Historical Sketch of the Southern Pacific*. Transcribed and edited by Bruce. C. Cooper. San Francisco: Southern Pacific Bureau, 1946.

Hernández, Sister María Victoria, O.P. *Ministry Under Fire: The First Foundations of Mexico Researched and Compiled*. Mission San Jose, CA: Dominican Sisters' Printing, 2002.

Inasmuch as Ye Have Done It unto One of the Least of These. Duarte, CA: Santa Teresita Guild, 1948.

Kelley, Most Reverend Francis Clement. *Blood-Drenched Altars: A Catholic Commentary on the History of Mexico*. Rockford, IL: TAN Books, 1987.

Kennedy, Sister Timothy Marie, O.C.D., ed. *In Love's Safekeeping: The Letters and Spiritual Writings of Mother María Luisa Josefa of the Most Blessed Sacrament*, vols. 1 and 2. Alhambra, CA: Carmelite Sisters' Printing, 1999.

Kenny, Michael, S.J. *No God Next Door*. New York: William J. Hirten Company, 1935.

Laurentius, J. "Diocesan Chancery." *Catholic Encyclopedia*. New York: Robert Appleton, 1908. http://www.newadvent.org/cathen/04798c.htm.

Bibliography

Markel, Howard, and Alexandra Minna Stern. "The Foreignness of Germs: The Persistent Association of Immigrants and Disease in American Society." *Milbank Quarterly* 80, no. 4 (December 2002): 757–788.

Martinez, Sister Mary Gonzaga, O.C.D., trans. *A Biography of My Beloved Aunt, Mother María Luisa Josefa of the Most Blessed Sacrament.* Alhambra, CA: Carmelite Sisters' Printing, 2005.

Meyer, Jean A. *The Cristiada: El Conflicto Entre el Estado y La Iglesia.* Delegación Coyoacán, Mexico: FCE-Clío, 2012.

———. *The Cristiada: The Mexican People's War for Religious Liberty.* New York: Square One Publishers, 2013.

———. *The Cristero Rebellion: The Mexican People between Church and State, 1926–1929.* London: Cambridge University Press, 1976.

Neumayr, George. "The 'Private Idea' of Parental Rights." *Crisis Magazine*, April 11, 2013. https://www.crisismagazine.com/2013/the-private-idea-of-parental-rights.

"Anti-clericalism." *New World Encyclopedia.* http://www.newworldencyclopedia.org/entry/Anti-clericalism.

Orozco y Jiménez, Right Reverend Francisco. "Why I Became an Exile." *The Little Flower Magazine* 12 (1930).

Original Letters of Father Jose Refugio Huerta to Mother Luisita. Compiled by Sister Mary Jeanne Coderre, O.C.D. Alhambra, CA: Archives of the Carmelite Sisters of the Most Sacred Heart of Los Angeles, 2002.

Original Letters of Father Pedro Heriz, O.C.D. to Mother Luisita. Compiled by Sister Mary Jeanne Coderre, O.C.D. Alhambra, CA: Archives of the Carmelite Sisters of the Most Sacred Heart of Los Angeles, 2001.

Original letters to Mother Luisita from Brother Gregory Mallon, F.S.C., and Brother Ralph McKeever, F.S.C. Archives of the Carmelite Sisters of the Most Sacred Heart of Los Angeles.

Parsons, S. J. *Mexican Martyrdom, 1926–1935: Firsthand Experiences of the Religious Persecution in Mexico.* Rockford, Illinois: TAN Books, 1987.

Positio Super Virtutibus: Canonizationis Servae Dei Maríae Aloisiae Iosep-hace a SS. Sacramento. Rome: Tipografia Guerra, 1991.

Queen, William M. *The Doctor's Widow.* Fresno: The Academy Library Guild, 1956.

Ruiz, Ramón Eduardo. *Triumphs and Tragedy: A History of the Mexican People.* New York: W.W. Norton, 1993.

Sánchez, George. *Becoming Mexican American: Ethnicity, Culture and Identity in Chicano Los Angeles, 1900–1945.* Oxford: Oxford University Press, 1993.

Saunders, Father William. "The Use of Sacramental Oils." *Arlington Catholic Herald.* Reprinted at Catholic Education Resource Center. http://www.catholiceducation.org/en/culture/catholic-contributions/the-use-of-sacramental-oils.html.

Sullivan, Reverend Philip, O.C.D. Interview with author. Alhambra, California, October 20, 2015.

Viva Cristo Rey! A Compilation of Articles on the Persecution of the Catholic Church in Mexico. Compiled by Sister Mary Jeanne Coderre, O.C.D. Alhambra, CA: Carmelite Sisters' Printing, 2007.

Williams, Fred V. "Carmelites Grateful for St. Mary's Offer." *Monitor,* May 12 and June 3, 1928.

Witness of a Charism: Personal Testimonies of Mother María Luisa Josefa of the Most Blessed Sacrament. Compiled by Sister Joseph Louise, Padilla, O.C.D. Alhambra, CA: Archives of the Carmelite Sisters of the Most Sacred Heart of Los Angeles, 2016.

About the Author

Sister Timothy Marie Kennedy, O.C.D., is a member of the Carmelite Sisters of the Most Sacred Heart of Los Angeles. She was born and raised in Long Beach, California, the third of five children. Sister Timothy attended Mount St. Mary's College in Los Angeles and has a B.A. in English and an M.S. in educational administration. She has served in the retreat and education ministries of the Carmelite Sisters as retreat directress, vocation directress, teacher, and principal in various schools. She is currently residing at Loretto Convent in Douglas, Arizona.

Sister Timothy edited the two-volume set of the letters of Mother Luisita, the foundress of the Carmelite Sisters, *In Love's Safekeeping: the Letters of Mother Luisita*. Sister Timothy comes from a family of Irish writers and storytellers.

Sophia Institute

Sophia Institute is a nonprofit institution that seeks to nurture the spiritual, moral, and cultural life of souls and to spread the Gospel of Christ in conformity with the authentic teachings of the Roman Catholic Church.

Sophia Institute Press fulfills this mission by offering translations, reprints, and new publications that afford readers a rich source of the enduring wisdom of mankind.

Sophia Institute also operates two popular online Catholic resources: CrisisMagazine.com and CatholicExchange.com.

Crisis Magazine provides insightful cultural analysis that arms readers with the arguments necessary for navigating the ideological and theological minefields of the day. *Catholic Exchange* provides world news from a Catholic perspective as well as daily devotionals and articles that will help you to grow in holiness and live a life consistent with the teachings of the Church.

In 2013, Sophia Institute launched Sophia Institute for Teachers to renew and rebuild Catholic culture through service to Catholic education. With the goal of nurturing the spiritual, moral, and cultural life of souls, and an abiding respect for the role and work of teachers, we strive to provide materials and programs that are at once enlightening to the mind and ennobling to the heart; faithful and complete, as well as useful and practical.

Sophia Institute gratefully recognizes the Solidarity Association for preserving and encouraging the growth of our apostolate over the course of many years. Without their generous and timely support, this book would not be in your hands.

www.SophiaInstitute.com
www.CatholicExchange.com
www.CrisisMagazine.com
www.SophiaInstituteforTeachers.org

Sophia Institute Press® is a registered trademark of Sophia Institute.
Sophia Institute is a tax-exempt institution as defined by the
Internal Revenue Code, Section 501(c)(3). Tax I.D. 22-2548708.